Send
My
Roots
Rain

Send My Roots Rain

A Study of Religious Experience in the Poetry of Gerard Manley Hopkins

Donald Walhout

OHIO UNIVERSITY PRESS | Athens   London

Library of Congress Cataloging in Publication Data

Walhout, Donald.
    Send my roots rain.

    Bibliography: p. 198
    Includes index.
    1. Hopkins, Gerard Manley, 1844–1889—Criticism and
interpretation. 2. Hopkins, Gerard Manley, 1844–1889—
Religion and ethics. 3. Experience (Religion) in literature. I. Title.
PR4803.H44Z917   821'.8   80-23549
ISBN 0-8214-0565-9

To Justine

Preface

In 1927 the *Cambridge Book of Lesser Poets* devoted one page, page 443, to Gerard Manley Hopkins and included there only one poem, "Heaven-Haven." This single entry was placed, may I emphasize, among *lesser* poets not *greater* poets. If anyone had made a forecast of obscurity for Hopkins based on that fact, such a prediction could hardly have been more wrong, as evidenced by the quantity of Hopkins studies of many kinds produced in the fifty years since that anthology was published.

And yet, despite this enormous interest, no full-length study of the structure of religious experience characteristically informing Hopkins's poetry has been made, even though everyone recognizes the importance of religion in his poetry. The present work is a study of this kind. The author, however, is a philosopher, not a literary critic, so there will be few literary matters attended to for their own sakes. My interest is rather the phenomenology of religion as disclosed in literature.

The book, more specifically, deals with the analysis and interpretation of what I take to be the predominant type of religious experience reflected in Hopkins's poetry. This experience is not that of the religious seeker but that of the already committed individual, namely, the experience of postcommitment desolation and recovery. This experience contrasts markedly with other types of religious experience, such as conversion, worship, or mysticism. This study also contrasts markedly with other treatments of Hopkins, which have been chiefly literary, historical, and biographical. The study is called phenomenological because it seeks to identify, describe, and interpret the inwardly felt states and stages of the experience in question.

The experience appears in three stages, which are called encagement, naturation, and grace. Encagement suggests a sense of entrapment, which is the central condition leading to desolation. Naturation refers to those means of recovery which are open to human effort. Grace indicates the culmination of recovery through felt divine initiative. Hopkins's portrayal of this type of experience has, I suggest, far more general relevance for the illumination of contemporary religious life than might be supposed by someone who focused solely on the local Jesuit context out of which the poetry came. The experience was certainly known to Loyola, to the author of *The Imitation of Christ*, and to others; but Hopkins gave unique and universal expression to it in poetic form.

This central experience and the way it is approached are introduced in chapter one as foreground. The next three chapters then dissect, respectively, the three stages of the experience and document their components from Hopkins's verse. This analysis is done, as far as is feasible, without reference to Hopkins's life. But later, in chapter five, Hopkins's life is discussed as a primary illustration of the religious phenomenology just surveyed. Two patterns in the experience are examined in his life—a definite, short-term, cataclysmic pattern, and a more chronic pattern of continuous grappling with encagement and recovery.

In chapter six, various interpretations of this central experience and of Hopkins's account of it are examined critically. Two main problems are discussed—that of the cause of the experience and that of how to classify it essentially. A plurality of natural causes, physical and mental, seems to be at work in the experience; and spiritual causation must also be assumed if the experience is held to be nonillusory. This last point is explored further at the end of the chapter. The ways of classifying, and therefore interpreting, Hopkins's account of the experience are divided into nonreligious and religious interpretations. The conclusion of this examination of views is that the central experience, with its three stages, is best thought of as a distinct type of religious experience, not as a variant of some other.

Chapter seven discusses, as background, Hopkins's philosophical views on religion. Besides this main function of the chapter, it also has the function of showing a side of Hopkins seldom met, namely, his philosophical interests.

Finally, in an epilogue, I elaborate the thesis that the illumination drawn from this religious phenomenology is the chief personal legacy of Hopkins's religious poetry.

Several points about sources are in order here. The following abbreviations will be used in footnotes for the six major volumes of Hopkins's writings (full citations are listed in the bibliography):

Poems refers to *The Poems of Gerard Manley Hopkins*, fourth edition;

Letters refers to *The Letters of Gerard Manley Hopkins to Robert Bridges*;

Correspondence refers to *The Correspondence of Gerard Manley Hopkins and Richard Watson Dixon*;

Further Letters refers to *Further Letters of Gerard Manley Hopkins, Including His Correspondence with Coventry Patmore*;

Journals refers to *The Journals and Papers of Gerard Manley Hopkins*; and

Sermons refers to *The Sermons and Devotional Writings of Gerard Manley Hopkins*.

The supreme bibliographical work on Hopkins is, at the present time, Tom Dunne's *Gerard Manley Hopkins; a Comprehensive Bibliography*. An excellent chronology of Hopkins's life can be found in Paul Mariani's *A Commentary on the Complete Poems of Gerard Manley Hopkins*, pages xi-xiv. This work also gives useful explanations of all the poems. *The Hopkins Quarterly* covers new bibliographical items and also discusses the current status of Hopkins biography, for example, in the Fall/Winter 1977/78 issue.

For various kinds of assistance I would like to offer grateful acknowledgment to each of the following: to the Ohio University Press reviewer for his or her unusually extensive and perceptive criticism which led to a greatly improved revision; to my family—Justine, along with Mark, Tim, Lynne, and Peter—for miscellaneous aid with the manuscript; to Ruth Seelhammer of the Crosby Library at Gonzaga University for her courtesy in permitting me to use the Hopkins Room during a research visit in 1975; to Rockford College for several small grants; to Dr. Dain Trafton, Chairman of the Rockford College English Department, for several suggestions and for his general encouragement of work in the humanities; and to Janet Nelson for secretarial aid.

Contents

CHAPTER *I*

The Central Experience
in Hopkins's Poetry

THIS BOOK has as its focus a certain type of religious experience disclosed in the poems of Gerard Manley Hopkins. In this opening chapter I shall, first, outline some general points of orientation for the study; second, present a preliminary characterization of the experience to be studied; third, compare some earlier accounts of the experience which are analogous to Hopkins's account; and last, offer some interpretive remarks on the importance of this theme in Hopkins's poetry.

1. *Theme and Approach*

The type of experience in this study has been little enough treated by either poets or religious writers, even though it is recognized in religious tradition. Yet the experience is, I believe, far more pervasive in contemporary life than might be suggested by its literary neglect.

The experience here is not the experience of the convert undergoing the throes of painful transition, though that too is intimated in Hopkins's poetry. It is not the experience of the spiritual pilgrim or wanderer trying to find a home in a world that ever foils his search. It is rather a postconversion experience or an experience that occurs after a commitment has been firmly made. Moreover,

1

the experience is not to be described as that of natural spiritual growth and maturing, or steady intensification of spirit, or santification of an original faith, though this aspect of religion is also present in Hopkins. The topic is rather the experience of desolation, barrenness, and spiritual dryness, together with the recovery therefrom, that may befall the spiritually committed person. This experience is not the doubt of the skeptic, not the confusion of an unchosen direction in life, not the hollowness of hollow men. The experience in this study is a potential hazard that comes not prior to, but subsequent to and consequent on, spiritual affirmation. And yet the very spiritual commitment itself contains the seeds of recovery from the desolation, though it does not automatically eliminate all feelings of barrenness and despair. It is this complex experience of postcommitment desolation and recovery, dryness and rain, that Hopkins reveals with such power. Its phenomenology, stage by stage, and the interpretation of it, is the subject here.

That there are various types of religious experience seems quite clear both from common observation and from the extensive literature on the subject, from James's *Varieties of Religious Experience* onward. It is important to mention this variety in order to emphasize that this study is of limited scope as far as religious phenomenology is concerned. Already cited as types of religious experience have been conversion, the journeyings of spiritual pilgrimage, and growth in spiritual maturing. Another type is the natural joyousness that James called the state of the "once-born" individual, which apparently takes place without conversion or darkness. There are also the typologies of various mysticisms, mild and full, Eastern and Western. In contrast to these, there are the typologies in monotheistic religion of worship and adoration and of prophetic calling and spokesmanship. Other awarenesses of the holy, or of sacred power, may be less institutionalized. It is not to the point here to attempt a detailed listing or classification of the various typologies that religious phenomenology could investigate. My point is merely that, from among these many forms, I shall concentrate on that one which dominates Hopkins's mature poetry, namely, the experience of postcommitment desolation and renewal.

I shall not deny that there are, in the extant poems of Hopkins, other expressions of religious experience besides those of the dominant type. His references to conversion, his pure celebrations of divine "instress" into nature, his offerings of adoration to God, and his doctrinal utterances would be illustrations. I claim only that the dominant type is just that—dominant—not that it is all-inclusive. However, I believe that the other religious emphases in Hopkins, except perhaps the doctrinal pieces, are for the most part best understood when taken as integral with the dominant type. There is then a more unified typology than might be suspected from merely looking at the poems disparately. This claim seems reasonable not only because of the inherent clarity of the religious typology that stands out in the poems, but also because the basic poems dealt with here come from a postcommitment setting in Hopkins's own life, a time long after he underwent conversion to Roman Catholicism and faithfully accepted the Jesuit order. That is, despite their diversity, the basic poems emerged chronologically from postcommitment experience and can thus be viewed as unified in this respect as well.

Someone might think that the emphasis I propose will stress too much the despair and desolation theme as drawn from the ten or so despair sonnets of Hopkins's last years, from about 1885 to 1889, when he was admittedly in a weakened condition. But such will not be the case. One could argue, of course, that these despair poems are extremely powerful statements and self-proclaim their own prominence regardless of anyone's emphasis. More to the point is the clear indication that the despair and desolation theme appears earlier as well. Even in the nature poems of 1877, such as "The Caged Skylark" and "The Sea and the Skylark," there are intimations of the spiritual problem that is a key element in the experience. Moreover, despair, although a profound element in the experience, is not the only element, and it will not be dwelt on at the expense of recovery.

If this study is selective among types of religious experience, selective as well among topics in Hopkins's poetry, it is also selective among studies of Hopkins. Its interest is not, for example, biographical in any direct sense. The concern here will not be with the chronological development of the poet's own personal experience but with a general phenomenology of experience exhibited in the poems themselves. To be sure, the distinction can hardly be rigid. Obviously the most vivid instance of the general pattern will be the poet's life out of which the poems have sprung, and in chapter five I want to portray that illustration specifically. Allusions to Hopkins's life will occasionally illuminate the traits in the general typology as the study proceeds; but biography is not its principal focus.

One significant difference between the phenomenological and the biographical approaches is in the handling of the chronology of the poems. Biographically, the first poetic outburst of Hopkins, after "The Wreck of the Deutschland" and after he felt free to return to poetry following his original vow to leave it, consisted mainly of nature poems. Then followed poems on human themes and other religious topics. Only toward the end of his life does one find the explicit, intense outcries of depression and desertion. Biography would describe this chronology in detail. But from a phenomenological point of view the problematic situation of depression and despair comes topically first in the typology. That is, there is a characteristic problem and a characteristic solution in the typology, regardless of the order of poetic composition in Hopkins's career. The study will therefore range over the entire body of poems to articulate the pattern involved, without proceeding year by year or by some other chronological classification of the poems. It is my thesis that the poems do indeed reveal such a type of religious experience, and my task will be to bring it out.

Nor is the study primarily literary, except in the redundant sense that any study of a major literary figure could be called literary. Much has been written about Hopkins's poetic style, his innovative devices, his contributions to modern poetry. I shall have nothing to add on these matters and in fact shall have no occasion to mention them. The interest here lies wholly with the substance, not the style, of Hopkins's poetry, and more particularly with that topic in the substance already demarcated. In this connection it will be relevant to touch somewhat upon some of Hopkins's ideas about poetic substance, such as inscape and instress, but only for their bearing on the religious typology and not for their influence on poetic technique. The focus is phenomenological, not literary.

Professor Todd Bender suggests that studies of Hopkins can be generally grouped under five headings:

> Most of the studies can be classified in one of five categories: (1) biographical studies of the relation of the two vocations, priest and poet, in Hopkins; (2) studies of ideological influences on Hopkins; (3) studies of stylistic influences on Hopkins' verse; (4) defini-

tions of Hopkins' peculiar terminology and ideas; and (5) exegesis of particular poems.[1]

I could perhaps add a sixth category: studies of Hopkins as part of the Victorian age. The present work does not fall, however, into any of these categories. Only a few philosophers, like James Collins,[2] have written anything at all on Hopkins, and among literature critics, only a few, like Professor J. Hillis Miller,[3] show affinity to the kind of approach in this book. Certainly in the above kinds of studies there is much included, often with great insight, about religion and religious experience in Hopkins. But such experience tends to be integral with these other interests. I, on the other hand, shall investigate a phenomenology of religious experience in its own right and as the sole topic.

By phenomenology I do not mean anything esoteric or anything as technically presuppositional as Hüsserl's method. Here it is simply the scrupulous effort to describe, impartially and objectively, and yet with empathy, inward experience as experienced. One writer has called it "the art-science of the personal."[4] Instead, one might speak of it as the philosophical art of disclosing the general structures of lived experience. The lived experience of persons is what is to be revealed, not, however, in the fashion of a diary but rather in the manner of general description and analysis. Now religious experience is, if anything, intensely and intimately lived, and so it is a fitting subject for phenomenological surveillance. In studying a phenomenology of religious experience in the poetry of someone like Hopkins, one has a profound and public source from which to draw the general description.

In presenting my account in the next three chapters, I shall find it useful to utilize segments and extracts from the poems and shall only occasionally examine poems in their entirety. This is because the concern here is with religious elements and not literary units. In this regard I am sensitive to the criticism that Paul Mariani makes of such a procedure when he finds it in Professor Miller's work. "There are," Mariani insists, "inherent shortcomings in a method which atomizes the poems for their paraphrasable content and then fuses them together into a new whole."[5]

Several points can be made in reply. First, different approaches to the same subject matter may be called for if the aims and interests of the inquiries are different. Mariani, from a literary point of view, wants to see each poem as a whole, and his commentary is devoted to that end. But if the aim of this study is to see general patterns cutting across the poems, then a more selective extracting may be appropriate. The two approaches are not incompatible.

I suspect that Mariani is as much opposed to the content of Miller's interpretation of Hopkins, centering as it does on the alleged disappearance of God in Hopkins, as he is to the methodology. If so, I am in full accord with Mariani, as will be shown in a brief discussion of Miller's view in chapter six. And if my interpretation of Hopkins is more in accord with Mariani's than with Miller's, then the case might be strengthened if it can be supported by a method more akin to that of the latter.

Furthermore, I believe one can use this extracting method without adopting the appraisal of Yvor Winters, who, in his low estimate of Hopkins, declares that "Hopkins is a poet of fragments for the most part, and it is only if one can enjoy a chaos of details afloat in vague emotion that one can approve the greater part of his work."[6] One need not hold that Hopkins is essentially a poet of fragments or his work essentially a chaos of details in order to hold that, for certain purposes, it may be very instructive to extract and juxtapose smaller literary units to exhibit common themes and structures.

I should add, independent of the above remarks, that no particular school of phenomenology, literary or philosophical, will be reflected here. Edward Cohen says of Miller's approach, "Prof. Miller, linked with the Geneva school of phenomenological critics, suggests that readers of poetry are not mere spectators, but participants whose realm of experience is within the subjective life of the poetic consciousness."[7] The last part of this quotation certainly suggests some common ground in phenomenology; but I have no link with any school of critics. I believe, in fact, that in philosophy phenomenology has come to designate, for the most part, an area of interest rather than any fully schematized method. That area of interest is lived experience, which one either undergoes oneself or identifies with in others. Some prefer the term "existential phenomenology" to distinguish this interest from the more original Hüsserlian interests and approaches. In either case the characterization given is sufficient for purposes of this study.

2. Elements in the Experience

But let me be more specific about the experience to be studied here. I shall do this by first introducing and commenting on the three central terms to be used in my analysis. These terms will be used to designate the three stages of the experience. I shall then give a capsule preliminary characterization of the experience as a whole, the elements of which will, in succeeding chapters, be dissected and illustrated from Hopkins' verse.

The first stage of the experience I shall call "encagement," a word I have coined from the meaning expressed in "The Caged Skylark," though it is by no means restricted in its exemplifications to that poem. Encagement is the spiritual problem of the postcommitment religious life that this study will be considering. It is a pervasive, spirit-depressing experience of binding confinement or overall containment. It may be spawned by frustration with one's immediate personal surroundings, or by a general sense of personal nonfulfillment, or by a deeper emptiness felt. Such encagement has consequential impact on one's emotional life and on one's attitudes toward other people, God, the world at large, and oneself. The various facets of this total experience will be distinguished in the next chapter and illustrated from Hopkins's poetry. Encagement is not usually associated with spiritual commitment, since the latter is thought to be precisely the condition that prevents or unshackles any encagement. But in Hopkins one sees clearly that the act of spiritual commitment, the upholding of vital conviction, the adherence to a chosen regimen, do not in themselves eliminate the finite conditions in which people must live their lives. Encagement is thus a possibility and often a reality.

The second stage of the experience I shall call "naturation," coining this word not from any specific locus in Hopkins but from his frequent attention to the created realm of nature and from his intimations of the significance of the natural world and of man's natural potentialities in a sound spiritual life. Nature, including human nature, has its own inherent laws, its own divinely intended processes, which, if man would but attend to them, could yield models of emulation and opportunities for restoration. Naturation, then, comprises the processes of incipient recovery, through natural means, from the original encagement and desolation. "Nature" in the narrower sense designates the physical world with its phenomena and laws. Hopkins showed much interest in this nature, of course, especially its individual beings. But "nature" in the wider sense, and as the root of "naturation," designates the whole created realm, including man, insofar as this realm can be considered to have its own ways and qualities in contrast to supernatural activity and being. This context is the one in which people speak of things occurring "by nature" in contrast to, but not opposed to, that which comes "by grace." Thus this term is related to the historic distinction between nature and grace. In man the "by nature" sphere includes his freedom, and so one can meaningfully ask about the earthly means and potentials that are open to man to contribute to his own natural recovery. The process of so doing is naturation.

The third stage in the total experience is the experience of grace. The term "grace" will be used to designate that dimension of the recovery from despair that is felt not as natural achievement but as a movement within oneself through a divine efficacy from beyond oneself. It is felt as power that restores despite one's own inabilities and ineptitudes. "Not I, but Thou that workest in me" is the characteristic sentiment. It is also felt as superseding and completing naturation, then as deepening and interpreting that earlier level of recovery. As is clear from this characterization, I shall be considering grace phenomenologically as a felt experience, not theologically as a divine attribute and the source of man's redemption. Furthermore, I do not want to suggest that grace is the last phase of three sharply distinct phases in an exact chronological sequence. There may be ups and downs, partial recoveries and reversals, in any given person's life, as in the life of Hopkins himself, and nature and grace may be felt interpenetratingly throughout the experience. But grace is certainly felt as the qualitative crown.

Encagement, naturation, grace—these are the three central terms employed in this study in analyzing this postcommitment experience of dryness and renewal. Eventually I shall refer to this experience as the ENG experience, pronouncing the symbol as distinct letters—E–N–G—similarly to ESP, though the two things have little else in common.

What follows next, then, in the remainder of this section, is a brief wholistic summation, a concentrated phenomenology, of the entire experience that I believe to be a unifying structure for understanding Hopkins's poetry.

It may come to happen in one's spiritual cultivation, one's religious vocation, one's relation to God, that one feels periodically encaged, like a skylark, whose natural home is free-winging air, confined in a cage that circumvents both flight and song. The problem is not one of doctrinal wandering, or of what religion to choose if any, or of ignorance of means of grace, or of nonparticipation in spiritual discipline. These things have been decided and, although always open to review in freedom, not rejected. The point is rather that life's circumstances—outward or inward, physical or mental—may temporarily overpower one's usual sensibilities, outdistance one's will, impoverish one's zeal, enclose one's endeavors, and effect a sense of inner incarceration. One feels thwarted, constricted, imprisoned. Life is circumscribed in gnawingly narrow bounds, tethered by tightening bands of constraint.

Or sometimes one feels a sense of personal nonfulfillment. One has talents, ambitions, aspirations; one has put forth efforts, striven for goals. But these aspirations and efforts are felt as unsuccessful and unfruitful. Talents are thus felt to be unused, desires unrealized, and hopes for achievement seem floundering. The land one might have cultivated lies fallow.

A sense of nonfulfillment may give way to a sense of barrenness and emptiness, which is a more radical sense of sterility in one's capacities. Nonfulfillments might be overcome by successes; but barrenness cannot yield a birth. One may come to think of oneself as a creative or contributory eunuch with nothing to produce or offer. One lives in a "winter world" in which nothing can grow. The vessel that one would like to have overflowing is inherently empty.

Three waves of emotional distress or dejection may set in: disappointment, discouragement, despair. Disappointment is a reaction to particular failures and frustrations. Discouragement is a more general dejection in face of a general inability to accomplish ends. Despair, in the ordinary and not the theological sense, is a pervasive depression based on a disappearance of hope in accomplishment or fruition. The entire emotional dryness accompanying encagement may be called desolation. The opposite is consolation: in the experience one does not feel the customary consolation of spiritual strength.

The religious believer relates such experience to God, and this relation makes his experience different from that of a secularist. In particular, the experience is seen as an absence of God. The bitterness of desertion may be uppermost in this reaction. Laments at a great loss may flow; reproaches may be hurled; even sarcasm or scoffing may escape. A questioning of God's ways may emerge and baffle one's reason. At the same time, supplications for relief and restoration are continued and intensified. And through it all one is able to accept the uncertainty and the chastisement, for one believes, however dimly, that somehow there is purpose in the absence. "Verily Thou art a God that hidest Thyself" but there may be design in the hiding.

A sense of desertion by God may be linked with a sense of isolation from other people. Overtly this sense of isolation could be a felt separation or distance from particular individuals whom one knows—family, friends, associates. It may expand into an isolation from all individuals, known or unknown. More deeply, it may be a sense of estrangement from all humanity, so that one feels inherently a stranger in the midst of mankind. This isolation is a potential consequence that has its roots in man's fallen condition.

The sorrows of encagement and emptiness, desertion and isolation, may gather into a more encompassing world-sorrow, a Welschmertz, which will be a kind of outer penumbra within which the dark central shadows of personal grief are located. A transition to this world-grief may be a lamentation over the spoliation of nature wrought by man. The roots of world-sorrow lie in transitoriness and death. Existence is temporal and changing and brings all achievements, momentary by nature, to an end. And our own frail life is no exception, so that we are moving from birth onward to the obliteration inherent in mortality.

The personal sorrows culminate, finally, in acute mental torture. Agony, anguish, and self-hate well up. Agony is excruciating pain, grating and grinding torment. Anguish adds the uncertainty of fearfulness, darkness, and comfortlessness. Self-hatred adds a sense of being unworthy and despicable.

Such is the pattern of encagement and desolation. Yet healing is possible. The spiritually committed person sees resources and has hope. Some of the resources are open to his own hand, made possible as gifts of his nature. The rest, and the ultimate hope, are from God's grace.

First, what can man do himself? What are the resources in that renewal that we can call naturation?

One healing power is beauty. Man can be open to beauty. Beauty sometimes directly drowns despair; it can yield a rich refreshment through the individuality in existing things; it can draw one toward and into goodness; it can help to heighten moral responsibility; it can bring ecstasy in a time of sorrow. Beauty, for Hopkins, is objective and universal in being and so is a potential in itself not limited to subjective intention. One can turn to it in nature. One needs to remember, however, that beauty can be distractive and beguiling, and it must be seen as pointing to a "better beauty, grace." With this caution, one can find beauty almost everywhere, both in natural things and in human form, and beauty's balm can belong to everyone who is in distress. He need only meet it and accept it.

Closely related to the appreciation of beauty is one's own creative activity. Creativity too is healing. Art, for instance, in accenting individuality in form, speaks to the individuality in man and brings out the true individual self. Its sense of abandon speaks to the latent freedom in the encaged self. Even though encagement and desolation are what stifle creative expression, still the nature of man contains ever the potentiality for breaking into healing artistries.

Moral resolve is also a restorative influence. It is part of the natural law tradition that man has the natural strength and practical reason to undertake moral endeavors on his own. One can begin with what is immediately urgent—the desire to stay alive, to keep going, to hope for relief, to do tasks at hand. One may then be in a position to impel oneself into wider duties in one's calling and even to accept, or renew, responsibilities regarding others, the community, and society. In the end one may even feel enabled to interpret the desolation itself as at least having the positive benefit of chastening and bolstering one's moral resolve.

An early result of moral resolve is likely to be the ability to do daily work, which itself has remedial value apart from fulfilling a sense of duty. The ability to do one's work is often a casualty of depression; so, inversely, if one can manage to work, the performance of daily work can be healing. It can organize time, deflect self-pity, and afford a sense of contributing. Man, created as a being of dignity and worth, brings dignity thereby to the constructive work he does. Thus to celebrate daily work is to acknowledge this human dignity, and participation in daily work can help to restore a sense of worth to one's troubled soul.

Human association, so often taken for granted, is a special balm in times of desolation and may be the only real, solid comfort left at such times. To care about another, and to feel that another cares about oneself, is a ladder of restoration with solid rungs even if one is not climbing. Hence another thing one can do is keep alive and expand the human contacts possible to him. It is possible to feel this support from any degree of acquaintance, from the most distant to the most known, and from any degree of comradeship, from the slightest to the most intimate. The closer the fellowship, the stronger the support; but one can find comfort in fellow feeling with others, in general, with strangers, with those in need or those in special or interesting circumstances, or with people in various walks of life. Appreciation of all and felt association seem to be the keys.

The practice of spiritual discipline can also have therapeutic effects. Therapy is not its main purpose, since Hopkins holds with Christian tradition that spiritual discipline is a service to God and an honoring of him, and not, as some have conceived of religion, a self-induced ego-satisfaction. Nevertheless, if one is able to persist in it for the right reason, there may be psychological byproducts of a very beneficial sort. Spiritual exercises may thus forestall aimlessness of purpose, may circumvent wasteful brooding, may bring bodily and mental refreshment, may bring a consolation through the conviction of being oriented in a worthy direction. This sense of refreshment, may be the most immediately felt aspect of the discipline insofar as it is seen as a part of naturation. A more realistic and sober cognition will be that the cost and sacrifice of discipline are the precondition of some natural goods and the price one must pay for them. A still deeper realization will be the conviction that, even though natural goods and effects are wanting, spiritual discipline is necessary for that preparedness, for that dispositional readiness, of the soul to receive the higher graces if they are forthcoming.

Humor can be a cheering addition to the other primary methods of naturation. It can bring some gaiety into gloom, some detachment from self-absorption, some comic transcendence of one's too-wallowing wailing. It can make its contribution to a more wholesome attitude of good cheer and self-acceptance. It is among man's natural gifts and is available in times of disheartenment.

So encagement can be partly broken by natural means. But grace must abound for the process to be completed. What man can do by nature passes into what man receives by grace. Theologically, grace is a free, personal bestowal of unmerited favor upon man by God. Phenomenologically, it is felt as strength from beyond oneself, as an unexpected gift, as a renewal of spirit, as a response of deep gratitude.

Grace may be felt first as a powerful resistence to evil. At the most basic level, grace is a guard against the tendency during desolation simply to give up entirely and merely stagnate in emptiness. Something from beyond keeps one going. In addition, strength is afforded that can counteract specific temptations and evils. If these forms of privation are overcome, positive virtues are instilled by grace. Hopkins speaks especially of patience and love. This coping with evil is seen by the experient not as self-heroism but as divine action.

With elemental privations overcome and integrity in one's being maintained, one may begin to see purposes at work in one's suffering and to interpret it accordingly. The immediate purpose is felt to be that of enabling one to discover God afresh or in a deeper way. To this end the divine intention may also be seen to have a scourging function—rooting out barriers of guilt and hardheartedness; a winnowing function—removing chaff to leave pure grain; a teaching function—eliciting patience and other virtues; a directing function—turning a person away from passing frivolities to lasting goods; and a forging function—hammering out true selves as return presentations to God. These are inward impacts of the divine purpose. Its outward, universal aspect is seen to be simply God's accomplishing his own will in man, not because God is arbitrary power crushing all, but because his will is love and most worthy of being accomplished.

This perspective on divine purpose may now enable one to experience a new perspective on one's own calling and on the world as a whole. First, one may feel a newly inspired sense of mission in life. One's vocation, which perhaps had become a burden during desolation, may now be lifted up to a new significance by being seen as serving divine purpose. However lofty or humble one's work seems from human viewpoints, one feels that God's purpose is being carried forward in the time, the place, and the manner that one has been summoned to. This sense of calling, thus renewed, may have special meaning in the life of a religious; but it is clearly not limited to this kind of vocation. Any worthy vocation can be a vehicle for the grace of divine calling.

One may also see the larger world in a new light. Nature and man, from which and from whom one felt isolated during the throes of encagement, can now be celebrated as God's grandeur. Nature is extolled as God's very handiwork, bearing universally the marks of divine instress. And man, so justly censured for his sin and selfishness, can now be seen also for his truer self, the original being that is good and meant for noble stature. The creation is once again taken to glorify and not malign the creator.

Beyond these graces for daily life and thought comes a resumed growth in spiritual sanctification. Central to this growth is a deepening awareness of God's presence and steadfastness despite all trials, discouragements, or setbacks. His steadfastness may be felt as patience with our indifference, as mercy toward our follies, as concern for our rescue, as providence over specific events, as a preservation of our true selves, as sustenance of the whole natural order, as a reaching out to us even in the depths of oceanic darkness.

For the Christian experient of grace, a growing personal identification with Christ is a further dimension of sanctification. A desire to mirror his likeness increases. This experience may focus on a theological interpretation of Christ, or on taking Christ as a moral example, or on simple allegiance. Whatever the particular focus, Christ is emulated more and more as the central light and model.

The whole experience of grace culminates in a joyfulness of spirit that transcends the earlier grief. The sorrows of despair give way to a radiance of positive spiritual affections. These affections are addressed to God in grateful response for his mercy. This joy now vitalizes one's earthly career as life presses onward poised between precarious human realities and ultimate anticipations. Joy is thus seen as an effulgence of the creation's "sweet being" and original purpose from the very beginning. To serve joyfully in that movement is now possible.

3. Some Comparisons

The experience we have sketched reminds us, at one plane, of the Psalmist, who knew both mourning and glorification. Job would be another Biblical witness. Some early commentators on Hopkins sought a connection between him and mystics like St. John of the Cross, chiefly because of the "dark night of the soul" phenomenon; but such accounts have proved questionable, as I shall elaborate in chapter six. The two religious writers who seem to have spoken most directly on the general type of experience and who were also close inspirational guides for Hopkins are Thomas à Kempis and Ignatius Loyola. I should like to quote some of their allusions to the experience by way of historical background.

Although *The Imitation of Christ* is largely concerned with individual sin and the overcoming of it in order to live a devout life, the desolation and recovery phenomena are clearly recognized. "To those who are well-versed in the ways of God," Thomas à Kempis says, "there is nothing new about this, nothing strange; the great Saints and the Prophets of old often suffered similar alternations of consolation and dryness of heart."[8] The *Imitation* even suggests that the experience is universal in the spiritual life: "I have never come upon anyone, however religious and devout, who has not sometimes experienced a withdrawal of grace, felt a cooling-off of his fervor" (II:9,7). The reason for this occurrence is partly that God is specifically testing an individual's faith, but partly also because all men live in a finite world, a temporary abode, an alien way station with vicissitudes and temptations. "It's surprising, isn't it, that man's heart can ever be really contented in this life, when he reflects seriously on his exiled state, on the many dangers his soul runs?" (I:21,1). One has therefore to expect such distresses and be prepared to cope with them. "Do you imagine you will always have spiritual comfort whenever you want it? That was never the way with my Saints; what *they* had was a world of trouble, trials innumerable, utter desolation" (III:35,3).

As far as the actual feelings in encagement are concerned, one may find one possible expression in these words: "What a half-hearted, careless state we must have fallen into, that we should have lost, so soon, our early enthusiasm; that we should be tired out, lukewarm, weary of life itself" (I:18,6). As an example of one factor instigating this state, the author focuses on the natural needs of man: "all these natural needs have their claim on him, and it makes a devout soul feel wretched and harrassed" (I:22,2).

Although the *Imitation* concentrates on the acceptance of divine grace as the true resolution of the downfall, a role for natural powers and efforts is also clearly recognized, and the devout are urged on in that regard: "Up with you, and set about it this instant; tell yourself, 'Now is the time for action; this is zero-hour, just the right moment for making something better of my life.' But you are feeling low, and finding things difficult? Why, that is the very opportunity you want, to win your spurs" (I:22,5). Most of the injunctions made are for moral improvement or for preparing to receive grace; but occasionally there is one that bears directly on the encagement experience as this study interprets it: "Do willingly whatever you can, as best you can and as seems best to you; do not give up attending to your soul on account of any dryness or mental torment you may feel" (II:7,1). Whatever the moral or spiritual lapses may be, an individual can turn these to advantage by developing the opportunities they generate for springing to a higher state. In this respect Thomas can even speak of the cultivation of what he calls "holy sorrow": "Well for you, if you can manage to clear all distractions out of the way, and concentrate on a single point—the exercise of holy sorrow....Strive hard to reach that goal; habit must be formed, if habit is to be overcome" (I:21,2).

In the end, however, it is divine grace that is essential for recovery from desolation and for a return to the steadiness of religion: "It's like this; when the grace of God comes to a man, there's nothing he can't do. When it leaves him, he becomes poor and unsteady, abandoned, as it were, to the lash of misery" (II:8,5). By comparison with grace, the natural means available to man now seem dwarfed dramatically:

I may have at my side good men, devout brethren, loyal friends; I may have holy books or beautifully written treatises, sweet-sounding chants and hymns; but it's little help they can give me, little spiritual zest, when grace has left me and I am alone with my poverty. At times like these there is no better remedy than patient self-abandonment to the will of God.

(II:9,6)

It is almost as if Thomas were saying that the natural means are a necessary but not a sufficient condition for recovery—they cannot do the job alone; whereas grace is both necessary and sufficient—it is fully efficacious in itself.

There's no great hardship in doing without human comfort, so long as we have the comfort of God behind us; what *is* difficult—immensely so—is the ability to do without both, God's comfort and man's, the will to endure cheerfully having one's heart an outcast from happiness, to seek in nothing one's own profit and to have no regard for one's own merit. . . . The man who is carried by the grace of God rides pleasantly along; no wonder he feels no weariness.

(II:9,1)

The devout must realize grace as the ultimate source of renewal from their sorrow. "How can I bear this my life of sorrow, if you do not support me with your mercy and grace?" (III:3,7).

The Imitation of Christ is addressed primarily to those who undertake a disciplined religious life, usually in a monastic setting. So is Loyola's *Spiritual Exercises.* If, therefore, they lack the universality of a treatise on general religious phenomena or that of a poet's vision, it is remarkable that they nevertheless deal with conceptions that can so easily be extended to wider application. In Loyola's case, a special section is included dealing with desolation and consolation in the priestly life, and by implication, in the spiritual life generally as well.

First of all, for Loyola, consolation, as the preferred or ideal state of the soul, is defined as follows in the section called "Rules for the Discernment of Spirits":

I call that consolation when there is excited in the soul some interior movement by which it begins to be inflamed with the love of its Creator and Lord. . . . Likewise when it sheds tears, moving it to

the love of its Lord....Finally, I call consolation any increase of
hope, faith, and charity, and any interior joy which calls and attracts
one to heavenly things.[9]

But the bleakness of desolation is fully recognized as a hazard.
Desolation is defined as follows:

> I call that desolation which is contrary to what is set down in the
> third rule, such as darkness and confusion of soul, attraction toward
> low and earthly objects, disquietude caused by various agitations and
> temptations, which move the soul to diffidence without hope and
> without love, so that it finds itself altogether slothful, tepid, sad, and
> as it were separated from its Creator and Lord.[10]

The need of natural means for alleviation is much in evidence in
such a state of desolation. "Let him who is in desolation consider
how our Lord, to try him, has left him to his own natural powers to
resist the various agitations and temptations of the enemy." The
rule proposed for these natural efforts is this: "Although in desolation we ought not to change our former resolutions, it is nevertheless very profitable greatly to change ourselves in opposition to
the said desolation; as, for example, by insisting more on prayer and
meditation, by making our self-examination more searchingly, and
by increasing in some suitable manner our penance."

But as with the *Imitation,* it is grace that is alone sufficient.
Devotees must "intimately feel that it is not in our own power to
acquire or retain great devotion, ardent love, tears, or any other
spiritual consolation, but that all is a gift and grace of God our
Lord."

All this is not quite the way Hopkins states these experiences,
nor how the study will do so in interpreting him. But the similarities
are obvious. Reverend Martin D'Arcy brings out this affinity when
he comments on John Pick's notable book on Hopkins. The language
is Catholic, as in the phrase, "and all his saints," and I would question the phrase, "without its natural supports"; but the placement of
Hopkins with a tradition is helpful:

> I am so glad that Dr. Pick dismisses the superficial talk of mystic
> "dark nights" when discussing the somber sonnets of Hopkins' last
> years. They obviously fall into what is well known as the season of

dry and dark faith, a season during which most good people are deprived of all the old sensible delights they formerly enjoyed when thinking of God and all his saints. Faith is left without its natural supports and never wavers—and so prepares the way for a fuller dependence on God in hope and a greater union in charity.[11]

Among modern writers there has been no full-length treatment of the central experience in Hopkins's poetry. W.H. Gardner's landmark two-volume work, for example, while recognizing the importance of religious experience in Hopkins, does not analyze it in depth but concentrates on literary and biographical topics. Nevertheless, there is a remarkable passage in Gardner which I should like to quote, for in it are clearly identifiable the principal elements this study will be investigating, with a qualification perhaps in the case of naturation:

> Now Hopkins's "desolation" was the aridity, protest, rebelliousness, terror, resignation, self-pity, quasi-cynicism, self-reproach, self-disgust and renewed self-dedication of the just man of declared faith who felt that he had been deserted by his God and could not be sure why; yet his faith continued to assert itself in a persistent humility, an underlying and unshakable conviction *either* that it was he himself who in the first place had deserted God, *or* that God would, in His own good time and way, answer the cries and prayers of His servant and eventually resolve all doubt.[12]

The two contemporary writers on Hopkins whose works are, in my judgment, most akin to the kind of interest in our present study are J. Hillis Miller and Robert J. Andreach. Although both move in different directions from the present study, both seek a structured form of experience that underlies Hopkins's poetry. Miller's work is avowedly phenomenological; but he focuses on inscape as the thematic structure—inscape of self, of nature, and of Christ—and in the end his conclusions are, in my opinion, as much biographical and historical as phenomenological. His book, in fact, is part of a trilogy on recent literary history. Andreach seeks a structure of religious experience in its own right in the poetry,[13] as I too shall do. But he uses the ready-to-hand categories of Catholic mysticism— the purgative way, the illuminative way, and the unitive way—and while he does not see Hopkins as a mystic, this structure seems to me to give a somewhat forced rendering of the poetry. I shall have more to say on each of these approaches in chapter six in another connection. But one further topic remains for this chapter.

4. *Universality in Hopkins*

Earlier I said that this study is not chiefly biographical. But any study of Hopkins must comment, it seems, on the perennial question of how to interpret the relation between the priest and the poet in this intriguing figure. Should one say, as some early critics did, that the native poetic genius was inhibited, throttled, crushed, by the extremity of the priestly vows and the religious life? Or should one say that the religious life was the very soil out of which the poetry grew, so that the poetry is an integral outcome of that life? This question is a familiar one, and I mention it only to indicate the guiding presupposition I think reasonable on it and to get then into a wider question.

It is quite plain to me, looking at the poems from a phenomeno-logical standpoint, as distinguished from a biographical interest in Hopkins or a psychological interest in art production, that Professor John Pick, for example, is completely right in arguing for an integral, constructive relation between the poetry of Hopkins and the religious life of Hopkins.[14] It is impossible to view the content of this poetry as coming from anything else but an intensity of Christian experience. Remove this Christian experience and its concrete Catholic and Jesuit embodiments which Hopkins felt it entailed for his own life, and the content of the poetry, let alone its very occur-rence, would seem to be impossible. This is not a comment in literary criticism or an evaluation of the poetry; it is simply an inescapable impression of the experience conveyed in the poems.

One still needs to ask further, however, how many of Hopkins's specific commitments need to be assumed as actually informing the religious experience revealed in the poetry considered as finished work. That is, granted that the full Christian, Catholic, and Jesuit commitment must be accepted biographically as the particular context out of which Hopkins's poetry emerged, must one also assume that this entire complex is essential to the understanding, interpretation, and appreciation of the experience portrayed in the poetry? Since there can be differences of opinion here, perhaps we should distinguish between a maximal thesis and a minimal thesis on this question.

The maximal thesis would be that the full Christian, Catholic, and Jesuit conviction is needed, at least by empathy, for the requisite understanding, interpretation, and appreciation. The minimal thesis would be that it is the Christian experience which is essential to the typology, but not the specific Catholic and Jesuit elements, however essential these are for the understanding of Hopkins the man and the poet. A more positive way of saying this would be to say that the minimal thesis suggests a greater universality of the experience than the maximal thesis would allow. Now it may be that those who agree with Professor Pick on the priest-poet debate, as I do, would, if they were confronted with the distinction I have made, agree that the minimal thesis is sufficient for the phenomenology of the central experience in the poetry even though more is needed for the biographical-critical interest in Hopkins. In that case there would be no inconsistency in holding the minimal thesis for the phenomenological question and the maximal thesis for the biographical-critical question. In any case, the minimal thesis seems to me sufficient for understanding and interpreting the typology that concerns us here.

I admit there is somewhat of a parochial bias in this: I would not like to think that Protestants like myself are bound to miss two-thirds of the poetry's significance. But aside from this irrelevant point, it seems clear to me, from a careful inspection of the poems, that there is nothing essential in them—at least in that dimension of them in which the phenomenology that concerns us occurs—which demands to be interpreted as uniquely Catholic or Jesuit. And nowadays such a judgment might be, one would suppose, ecumenically welcome to Catholics. To be sure, there are some outrightly doctrinal pieces and other scattered allusions to what is specifically Catholic or suggestive of Jesuit regimen. But these appear to be phenomenologically incidental to the central experience and to be simply part of the local biographical context in which the articulation of the more universal Christian experience was accomplished. It is that universal Christian experience, albeit in only a limited aspect, that will be the focus of attention here.

When one goes beyond the Christian experience, out of which Hopkins wrote, and asks about the universality of the typology in reference to other traditions and world-views, he has, of course, quite another question. The specifically Catholic and Jesuit elements can easily be seen, in an ecumenical age and viewed phenomenologically, as incidental variations in a common type of Christian experience. But can the Christian experience in turn be considered incidental to a wider typology found in the poems? This assumption would be very doubtful and would stretch the meaning of the poems far beyond what they actually say and communicate. Hopkins is a Christian poet and cannot be read as simply a spokesman for some kind of general religiousness. Other poets express their religious traditions, and Hopkins does his.

What one can say, however, is that there is probably an analogous situation, a family resemblance, in other religious settings. Probably the cognate monotheistic faiths, Judaism and Islam, could feel a good deal of analogous sympathy with the experience that Hopkins expresses, because it is steeped in personal theism. In some sense this may be true in other faiths as well. No doubt the phenomena of spiritual dryness and recovery are universal occurrences wherever there is serious spiritual concern. So in that respect Hopkins may be considered a universal poet, just as others may be who are able to speak generally for mankind though their own individual situations are particular. On the other hand, the dryness and recovery might be felt and interpreted so differently in other faiths, say Buddhism or Hinduism, that one ought not to press the universality beyond that of a general human analogy. Another reason for this restriction is the profound centrality that the personal God of Christianity and the identification with Christ have for Hopkins in both the problem and the resolution.

Great poets, like great philosophers, are many-faceted in their thematic content and in their appeal. In this situation there is always a temptation to claim that one has discovered the true author, the real substance, the quintessential core. I shall hope not to make this mistake in the present study, for the presentation can hardly be said to be the only profitable way of approaching Hopkins. Still there may be a helpful corrective in the emphasis I make. When the distinctiveness of Hopkins has been alleged by some to consist of his stylistics and diction, by others his Victorian unrepresentativeness, by others his Catholic didacticism, just to mention a few claims, it may be refreshing to see Hopkins as portraying to the reader a very profound and very human phenomenology of religious experience, an experience in which all readers might personally participate or from which, in any case, they can usefully learn more about religious experience and more about the facets of Hopkins's poetry.

In the past sixty years numerous interpretations of Hopkins have emerged, some of them in the light of preconceived schools or ideologies. It is therefore instructive to scout around the references to Hopkins prior to his publication.[15] One of these, written only twenty years after Hopkins's death and nearly a decade before Robert Bridges brought out the first edition of Hopkins in 1918, identifies the spiritual problem in a way remarkably akin to the way soon to be developed in this study, though nothing is said of the resolution:

> We must surmise a great part of this last struggle; but it would seem to illustrate the spiritual phenomenon of *desolation* which has immersed so many a chosen soul. For full thirty years was St. Theresa in this desert land; where frustration reigns in all visible things, and to lose the life *without finding it again* seems the guerdon of superhuman effort.[16]

One dares not speak in this case of a primitive tradition prior to the rise of scholarship. But what he can say is that there may be early intimations of themes which criticism has not always adequately illuminated. Such a theme is here, I believe, in this book. It is Hopkins's poetic illumination of the very human experience of many and many a spiritual aspirant.

CHAPTER *II*

Encagement

THE ROOT source of the religious experience Hopkins discloses in his poetry is the sense of encagement. Encagement is an encircling bondage in life with all of its emotional torment. One might speak as well of spiritual dryness or discouragement or despair as the root source. Encagement, however, appears to be prior to the dryness, causally if not chronologically. No doubt there are other sources of spiritual dryness articulated in religious literature, but encagement appears predominant in the experience Hopkins reflects. Its component elements, therefore, should be differentiated and illuminated. I shall focus first on the initiating conditions of encagement, then on its emotional impact, its external consequences, and its existential climax.

1. The Initiating Conditions

For Hopkins, the immediate initiating conditions of the sense of encagement appear to be entrapment in one's life circumstances, the inability to fulfill one's talents and desires, and felt emptiness or barrenness in life. One should look at these conditions in turn. Their common core is the squeezing down of that humanity in man which craves flourishing.

Perhaps the most immediately felt condition of encagement is expressed in such synonyms as trapped, thwarted, imprisoned, caught, ensnared, hemmed in, held fast. Something in a person's life situation compresses him within insufferable bounds. Hopkins's poems do not offer any tabulation of possible life contexts that could initiate encagement. His own specific life circumstances in this regard are well known from his other writings,[1] though not so much from the poems. One may presume that wherever there is a stultifying mismatch between someone's actual life circumstances and his self-identity or expectations, encagement is a threat. In any given case, it might be that, through inner resources, sheer grace, or just plain habit, this entrapment would not be felt as a crushing grip. In Hopkins's poems, however, the experience is dire indeed.

The *locus poeticus* in Hopkins for this experience is "The Caged Skylark." This poem is customarily interpreted as being primarily about man's embodiment, that is, the union of his spirit with a body. This interpretation gains credence perhaps from the fact that the poem begins and ends with such an allusion. It begins:

> As a dare-gale skylark scanted in a dull cage
>   Man's mounting spirit in his bone-house, mean house, dwells—[2]

and it ends by saying that man will not be "distressed" when he lives with "his bones risen," that is, his resurrection body.

The theme of embodiment is certainly present and cannot be denied. But if it were the primary emphasis, there would be an incongruous simile or false analogy in the poem. The basic comparison is of course between the caged skylark's situation and man's situation. But what precisely is being compared? Is it the cage and the body, as might be supposed? Hardly—and for a very good reason: a cage is an unnatural, artificial place, a real prison, for a skylark, whereas a body is not an unnatural, artificial place, and not a prison, for man. A rigorous Platonic or Neo-Platonic view might say so, but not a Christian view in which man is a spirit-body unity. Such an analogy would be a false analogy were it the main emphasis.

The comparison lies elsewhere. It is between a skylark imprisoned in a cage and man trapped "in drudgery, day-laboring-out life's age." It is not the body but the condition of being caught in drudgery that is the prison for man. Just as a skylark, when caged, might be "beyond the remembering his free fells," so man, when trapped, may be limited to no more than "day-laboring-out life's age." This statement is quite explicit, and it is given support in the next lines by a comparison of reactions. Despite the fact that

> Both sing sometimes the sweetest, sweetest spells,
> Yet both drop deadly sometimes in their cells
> Or wring their barriers in bursts of fear or rage.

Why would man wring his barriers "in bursts of fear or rage?" Not because he has a body, especially when he has no idea of what it would be like without a body (unlike the skylark who knows very well what it is like without a cage). No, he wrings his barriers because man is caught in an existential trap. This trap is his encagement.

The sestet of the poem then stresses the resolution of the predicament. What the skylark needs most of all—and by implication man also—is a return to "his own nest, wild nest, no prison." Man's liberation from his prison of drudgery will be an existence that is "uncumbered." Then the poem closes with a final clarification, by way of a coda, that this liberated existence does not mean removal of the body but an existence in which the body is a full participant: "Man's spirit will be flesh-bound when found at best," for the body is no encumbrance as such.

So the poem is dominantly one of encagement not embodiment. Through simple yet stunning simile, Hopkins shows the encagement to which man is subject and the "uncumbered" state to which he, like the skylark, aspires. The sociological and psychological circumstances of the condition of entrapment would naturally be quite diverse for different persons; but phenomenologically, it is an experience of being confined, contained, cut off from one's real habitat, one's "own nest."

Many expressions of entrapment are somewhat indirect in Hopkins because he focuses directly on the felt consequences attending the condition. This study will take notice of many of these felt consequences shortly. A fairly direct statement appears in "To seem the stranger lies my lot." Hopkins first mourns his estrangement in life, especially from family and homeland. The poem then concludes by saying that

> ... what word
> Wisest my heart breeds dark heaven's baffling ban

> Bars or hell's spell thwarts. This to hoard unheard,
> Heard unheeded, leaves me a lonely began.
>
>   (*Poems*, no. 66)

To generalize, I interpret Hopkins as saying that the best things one can produce may end up being barred or thwarted, and therefore these works may simply remain bottled up within oneself without being publicly released, or if released, never acknowledged or appreciated. All this can leave a person with the isolation of one who feels he is a mere beginner despite years of aspiration and effort.

In another direct statement, in one of his last three poems, "Thou art indeed just, Lord," the poet focuses on the divine relatedness of his encagement but also indicates the power of its grip. Speaking to God, he says:

> How wouldst thou worse, I wonder, than thou dost
> Defeat, thwart me? Oh, the sots and thralls of lust
> Do in spare hours more thrive than I that spend,
> Sir, life upon thy cause.
>
>   (*Poems*, no. 74)

With a divine reference, the thwarting may be felt as a "holy thwarting," if one may speak thus; but it is none the less felt as bitter defeat, as unthriving stagnation.

One can get a counterview of entrapment by comparing "The Windhover" with "The Caged Skylark." In some respects they are antitheses: the latter expressing encagement, the former the freedom to achieve and master. "The Windhover" is mainly about Christ and will be relevant later. But in its first part it gives a rapturous account of a falcon's free and dazzling flight:

> High there, how he rung upon the rein of a wimpling wing
> In his ecstasy! then off, off forth on swing,
>   As a skate's heel sweeps smooth on a bow-bend: the hurl and gliding
>   Rebuffed the big wind. My heart in hiding
> Stirred for a bird,—the achieve of, the mastery of the thing!
>
>   (*Poems*, no. 36)

Here the heart is stirred at the free, unimprisoned, ecstatic, magnificent achievement of natural talents and potentialities. This feeling is the opposite of encagement. Would that man could be liberated from his encagement to be as the windhover is.

Being thwarted or imprisoned, then, is one condition resulting in encagement. Closely intertwined with it is another, the inability to realize one's natural talents, proper desires, or legitimate expectations and ambitions. Contexts will vary. Perhaps there is lack of opportunity; perhaps one cannot get working; perhaps a calling prevents other activities; perhaps there are too many demands. Whatever the context, one feels that one's life as a human being is not being fulfilled adequately. The longed-for fruition is somehow sealed off, bringing a sense of encagement.

In *"Patience,* hard thing!" Hopkins has an apt phrase for this experience when he says that "patience masks our ruins of wrecked past purpose" (*Poems*, no. 68). The "ruins of wrecked past purpose"— that is how nonfulfillment may be felt. A person may have had some purpose, some intention, some ideal, rudely wrecked, leaving his desired fulfillment in ruins.

The two late poems already quoted also intimate this condition of unrealized potential. The estrangement poem beginning "To seem the stranger lies my lot" conveys throughout the sense of falling short that one can feel in relation to what might be or should be. From Ireland Hopkins can say, in more than one sense, "Now I am at a third remove," using the Platonic phrase that indicates the unreality of things compared with their true form.

Even more in "Thou art indeed just, Lord," one finds a vivid rendering of nonfulfillment. Following his protest to God over his condition, the poet compares his own futile efforts with nature's fruition—a frequent contrast in Hopkins:

> ... See, banks and brakes
> Now, leaved how thick! laced they are again
> With fretty chervil, look, and fresh wind shakes
> Them; birds build—but not I build; no, but strain,
> Time's eunuch, and not breed one work that wakes.
> Mine, O thou lord of life, send my roots rain.

The creatures of nature may perfect their ways smoothly and rhythmically; but man, despite all his struggle and strain, may not be able to build at all, may remain a eunuch in his endeavors, may not produce anything that matters.

Almost everyone believes he has some gifts, however modest, and so almost everyone is subject to nonfulfillment. Gifts may be either secular ones (such as those of artist, thinker, or practical person) or spiritual ones, of which St. Paul speaks. Nonfulfillment threatens spiritual gifts as well as secular ones. In "The Candle Indoors," this note is sounded. Seeing a candle in a window while passing by, the poet is prompted to hope that the tasks being done inside will glorify God. But this thought in turn prompts him to look inward to his own spiritual state instead of outward.

> Come you indoors, come home; your fading fire
> Mend first and vital candle in close heart's vault:
> *(Poems*, no. 46)

What once was a spiritual fire in man may have become a smoldering ash, and there may be no vitality left in the heart. Then, with biblical imagery, Hopkins continues the self-examination:

> What hinders? Are you beam-blind, yet to a fault
> In a neighbor deft-handed: Are you that liar
> And, cast by conscience out, spendsavour salt?

Spiritual strength may be reduced to fault-finding and self-deception; spiritual salt may lose all its savor and seasoning power. Hence, spiritually as well as secularly, one's best efforts, desires, and abilities may come to little or nothing, generating the encagement he is in.

In a youthful poem, "See how spring opens with disabling cold," Hopkins attributes this fallowness, at least one experience of it, to youthful indecision. It is not my intention to investigate factual causes of the phenomena surveyed here. Also one must be doubly careful not to take such a passage to imply anything biographical about Hopkins the mature priest. I repeat that I am not using any of the poems in this and the next two chapters for biography but only for phenomenological truths and insights. A study of the youthful poems must proceed with double caution in this regard. With these precautions in mind, however, one may look on the passage, not as a causal explanation, but as one expression of the feeling of frustration in nonfulfillment.

> It is the waste done in unreticent youth
> Which makes so small the promise of that yield
> That I may win with late-learnt skill uncouth
> From furrows of the poor and stinting weald.
> Therefore how bitter, and learnt how late, the truth!
>
> (*Poems*, no. 17)

Not only can one feel unfulfilled in one's abilities, desires, and efforts, but one may come to feel that one is an empty person, a completely barren individual. One feels a hollowness, an incapacity, a creative sterility. This barrenness is a deeper, more pervasive, more tenacious condition. Nonfulfillment could, after all, be viewed as merely temporary nonsuccesses of particular efforts or talents, which might be reversed by successes. But in this further mode of experience, one feels an incapability for success, a barrenness preventing any achievement. One is an empty person without the wherewithal for fulfillment.

The depth of this emptiness is evident in the images that Hopkins uses, which we have already encountered: "time's eunuch" and "a lonely began." A eunuch is not merely one who has not produced anything but one who is incapable of producing anything. By metaphorical extension, this expression means one feels that one is unable to be a productive person. And as "a lonely began," one feels that he is forever and necessarily a mere beginner. One is not the sort of person who can be anything but a novice, despite tremendous aspirations.

Hopkins's last poem, addressed to Robert Bridges and entitled "To R.B.," is his fullest account of the throes of emptiness. The reference is more personal than usual, explaining his own artistic barrenness. But it is clear that any person might feel himself in the same "winter world," a world in which flowering and growing are impossible. Paradoxically, the first half of the poem is a fine account of the nature of the creative process in art. Then follows the "winter world" lament:

> Sweet fire the sire of muse, my soul needs this;
> I want the one rapture of an inspiration.
> O then if in my lagging lines you miss
> The roll, the rise, the carol, the creation,

My winter world, that scarcely breathes that bliss
Now, yields you, with some sighs, our explanation.

(*Poems*, no. 76)

A person can, of course, sacrifice talent and creative endeavor to a higher calling, as Hopkins did earlier in his career; but that sacrifice would involve voluntary displacement and discipline. Far different is the sense of creative failure, of sterility in one's very capacities. To aspire and yet to feel barren, to conclude that one has nothing to offer—that is the condition of encagement here being revealed.

One finds a simple confession of this state in a fragmentary poem, "Trees by their yield," in which the metaphor of growing things is prominent, as it is so often and so appropriately in this theme of barrenness. A hint of cause and remedy is also present, though one can hardly take this as definitive in itself.

Trees by their yield
Are known; but I—
My sap is sealed,
My root is dry.
If life within
I none can shew
(Except for sin),
Nor fruit above,—
It must be so—
I do not love.

(*Poems*, no. 127)

Encagement, then, emerges from conditions of being trapped or thwarted, unfulfilled, or barren. It is a spiritual threat from which the spiritually minded person is not exempt on account of his spiritual interest or even his attained spirituality. Sieges of encagement may come to all, and all roots need rain.

2. The Emotional Impact

Turning to the emotional side of the experience, one finds that there are levels of intensity in the emotional disturbance caused by encagement. In increasing order of pain, three levels can be distinguished; they are called disappointment, discouragement, and despair. There are many other terms, many of them beginning with the letter *d*, that would serve as well. Some of these are: distress, defeat, dismay, depression, disheartenment, dejection, disillusionment, despondency, and, above all, desolation. This last word, desolation, will be used generally for the entire emotional spectrum of the experience whose various waves this study is isolating here and in other sections. That is, the feeling dealt with here is one of spiritual desolation caused by encagement.

Disappointment is the distress closest to the surface of awareness. It can be spoken of in the singular. A disappointment is a particular defeat felt from the failure of some hope, expectation, effort, or ambition. Disappointments can be reversed by countervailing successes in the same vein. If disappointments come regularly and seemingly perpetually, however—if, with Hopkins, one is led to wonder "why must disappointment all I endeavor end"—then disappointment may pass into a further level of distress.

Discouragement is a more general, pervasive, deep-seated disturbance in personal life. It represents a lack of confidence in one's endeavors, a feeling that disappointments are inevitable, a sadness in the inability to proceed with anything. It may become a relatively permanent state or disposition. A theological encyclopedia says of discouragement that it is a "general weakening of confidence, a disheartenment, a lessening of courage." Then the account continues: "This subject is of general interest to all who undertake long and arduous tasks and of special interest to those living a particularly spiritual type of life or those suffering from unusual periods of depression."[3] The description applies well to various states that Hopkins reveals in his poetry. But there is worse.

Despair is a still deeper condition. It is discouragement carried to the extreme of the disappearance of once-felt hopes and expectations. It is a deep-brooding sense of futility in the face of insurmountable obstacles. The previous source describes despair as "the abandonment of hope, entailing the rejection of some good as an object of efficacious desire because it is judged to be unattainable in the practical order."[4] This description is what one might call ordinary or emotional despair. In Catholic tradition, despair is also spoken of as one of the seven venal theological sins. In this sense, despair "as a *sin* consists in the relinquishing of present or possible hope. It is therefore the voluntary rejection of a consciously recognized dependence of man upon his fellowmen and upon God, as well as of the corresponding duties of seeking perfection and salvation in harmony with them."[5] It is important to distinguish these senses because it seems to me there is no evidence in Hopkins's poetry, or in other sources, that Hopkins himself was subject to despair in the theological sense, or that this kind of emotion is what is expressed in his poetry. He did not abandon belief in God, or reliance upon God, or the duties of the religious life, or the possibility of hope, or his love of fellowmen, or his spiritual regimen. Moving cries of despair appear in his poetry, but they express the ordinary or emotional despair that can well up in a person despite spiritual commitment and not a despair involving repudiation of the spiritual way of life. The preceding sentence in fact sums up the central problem with which this study is concerned—the desolateness that may befall even a person with steadfast spiritual orientation.

Hopkins's most explicit statement of disappointment can be found in the words quoted above from "Thou art indeed just, Lord." More fully, the idea is:

> Why do sinners' ways prosper? and why must
> Disappointment all I endeavor end?

In an earlier poem, "Peace," he expresses the restlessness, the ups and downs of spirit, which disappointment brings. This poem is of interest because it comes only two years after the exultant nature poems of 1877 and considerably before Hopkins's last Dublin depression, thus showing that the experience of which he writes is not a mere physiological quirk of his late years. He writes:

> When will you ever, Peace, wild wooddove, shy wings shut,
> Your round me roaming end, and under be my boughs?
> When, when, Peace, will you, Peace?—I'll not play hypocrite
> To own my heart: I yield you do come sometimes; but
> That piecemeal peace is poor peace. What pure peace allows
> Alarms of wars, the daunting wars, the death of it?
>
> (*Poems*, no. 51)

The discouragement wrought from repeated disappointments is voiced sharply in an unfinished sonnet. The context is a felt deterioration in civilization. "The times are nightfall," the poem begins. Every man faces "a world undone." Hopkins feels incapable of doing anything about it.

> And I not help. Nor word now of success:
> All is from wreck, here, there, to rescue one—
> Work which to see scarce so much as begun
> Makes welcome death, does dear forgetfulness.
> (*Poems*, no. 150)

One of the Dublin poems, "Spelt from Sibyl's Leaves," also using the imagery of night, expresses a similar gloom. Just as evening is passing into night, thereby obliterating the day's light and activity, so one's spiritual state, already dimmed, is threatened by further loss: "Heart, you round me right/With: Our evening is over us; our night whelms, whelms, and will end us" (*Poems*, no. 61).

If daytime is variable disappointment and success, if evening is a cloak of discouragement enwrapping us, the darkness of night is the final despair. In despair all seems hopeless and without light. Consolation wanes during despair and may fade to no more than the negative comfort of a possible end to it all, totally or at least for a day:

> ...Here! creep,
> Wretch, under a comfort serves in a whirlwind: all
> Life death does end and each day dies with sleep.
> ("No worst, there is none," *Poems*, no. 65)

Meanwhile, one does awake to another day, only to find that (to quote the title line of another poem) "I wake and feel the fell of dark, not day" (*Poems*, no. 67), and that life drags on sourly (to change the metaphor from the same poem): "Selfyeast of spirit a dull dough sours."

In "The Wreck of the Deutschland," whose religious phenomenology is rich and diverse, there is a statement of a direct correlation between encagement and despair. As the ship was sinking, a nun was heard to cry, "O Christ, Christ, come quickly" (*Poems*, no. 28: st. 24). But "what did she mean?" (28:25). Hopkins answers that it is not danger or the call for heroism that causes a person to desire release from life's distress and woe; rather, it is the drudgery of life's buffetings, the constant jading of life's career.

> The jading and jar of the cart,
> Time's tasking, it is fathers that asking for ease
> Of the sodden-with-its-sorrowing heart,
> Not danger, electrical horror.
>
> (28:27)

In "The Shepherd's Brow," despair widens from personal dejection to lament over the condition of mankind. Man's very condition is one of frailty and tragedy. This assertion is made in a comparison of man with angels and is marred only by an unfortunate pun.

> But man—we, scaffold of score brittle bones;
> Who breathe, from groundlong babyhood to hoary
> Age gasp; whose breath is our *memento mori*—
> What bass has *our* viol for tragic tones?
>
> (*Poems*, no. 75)

In "The Leaden Echo," a portion of a chorus for an unfinished verse play, the idea is suggested that despair is a structural feature of existence itself, an existential component of life, as if the confines of finite life form a generalized kind of encagement for all. Finite goods vanish, "And wisdom is early to despair" (*Poems*, no. 59). This emotional type of despair (though not the theological) is, then, an inherent hazard of life when life's bonds are seen from a purely natural standpoint. The poem continues:

> So be beginning, be beginning to despair.
> . . . .
> Be beginning to despair, to despair,
> Despair, despair, despair, despair.

3.   The External Consequences

Externally, encagement may engender a sense of alienation from personal sources of unity with God and other people. Of course these consequences are within the sufferer's experience and do not indicate a description of God and other people in themselves. That is, all phenomenology deals with inward experience rather than the outer world; but some of that experience points reflexively to the self and its states, and some to external relationships. This study will consider in turn these two external consequences—felt desertion by God and felt isolation from others.

To the spiritually committed person, encagement is seen in a necessary relation to divine reality. This relation is what makes it part of the total religious experience and why it cannot be omitted from the religious experience in favor of the positive renewal alone. Without this God-relatedness, after all, the other elements might be considered incidental episodes in a valueless universe, unfortunate but inevitable blemishes in an unfree man's worship. But for the spiritually committed, God remains somehow in the picture—if not in the foreground, at least in the background. The sufferer may wonder, doubt, rebel, curse, accuse, defy, disdain, brood, lament, languish—in relation to God. Yet God is not denied. Thus in some strange, mysterious, uncomprehended way, even desolation is of God.

There appear to be seven identifiable moments in this phase of the experience. The first and most elemental is the sense that one has been deserted by God: one feels abandoned. The second is lament and regret: one cries out in sorrow. The third is angry reproach: one lashes out against God, accuses him, or sarcastically scoffs at him. In the fourth stage, the heated emotion passes into sober questioning: one probes why one is being scourged in this way. A fifth moment is supplication: one implores for relief, strength, renewal. The sixth is realization of purpose in the encagement: one believes one is being chastised, cleansed, or tested in one's faith. Finally, there is acceptance: one is reconciled to the pain and purpose of the desolation. The last two moments belong to the resolution of the problem. The others are part of the encagement experience being analyzed in this chapter.

Desertion, lament, reproach, questioning, supplication—these one finds amid Hopkins's lines of spiritual dryness. A simple statement of God's absence is given in "No worst, there is none":

> Comforter, where, where is your comforting?
> Mary, mother of us, where is your relief?

These lines occur within a particularly poignant utterance of sorrow, a sorrow that is "pitched past pitch of grief." Yet the Holy Spirit, usually present, seems missing.

One of Hopkins's early poems, "Nondum," is devoted to this theme of God's absence. Admittedly from a time of youthful searching, it might likewise typify a temporary cry of a spiritually committed person. The poem is headed by the verse, "Verily Thou art a God that hidest Thyself,"[6] which appropriately indicates not only the sense of God's absence but also the spiritually committed person's belief that there is purpose, indeed a purposer, in the absence. It then proceeds:

> God, though to Thee our psalm we raise
> No answering voice comes from the skies;
> To Thee the trembling sinner prays
> But no forgiving voice replies;
> Our prayer seems lost in desert ways,
> Our hymn in the vast silence dies.
>
> We see the glories of the earth
> But not the hand that wrought them all:
> Night to a myriad worlds gives birth,
> Yet like a lighted empty hall
> Where stands no host at door or hearth
> Vacant creation's lamps appal.
>
> (*Poems*, no. 23)

Another early poem sounds the note of lament in these lines:

> My prayers must meet a brazen heaven
> And fail or scatter all away.
> . . . .
> I cannot buoy my heart above.
>
> (*Poems*, no. 18)

Returning to a late poem, "I wake and feel the fell of dark," poetically and spiritually more sophisticated, one finds this lament:

> ... And my lament
> Is cries countless, cries like dead letters sent
> To dearest him that lives alas! away.

There is not much reproachfulness in Hopkins. His poetry is too sophisticated, his life too dedicated, to engage in vindictive scoffing, which, after all, can be a little childish. Such reproachfulness as there is appears in "Thou art indeed just, Lord," the mature poem that is most directly devoted to the topic of God's desertion. The poem is prefaced by the opening, in Latin, of the twelfth chapter of Jeremiah: *"Justus quidem tu es, Domine, si disputem tecum: verumtamen justa loquar ad te: Quare via impiorum prosperatur? Ec."* In the Douay version, this reads: "Thou indeed, O Lord, art just, if I plead with thee, but yet I will speak what is just to thee: Why doth the way of the wicked prosper?"[7] A modern speech translation has it: "O Lord, You always give me justice when I bring a case before you to decide. Now let me bring you this complaint: Why are the wicked so prosperous?"[8] Hopkins's poem, first paraphrasing, then reproaching God for his condition of defeat despite devoting himself to God's cause, proceeds in part:

> Thou art indeed just, Lord, if I contend
> With thee; but, sir, so what I plead is just.
> Why do sinners' ways prosper?
> . . . .
> Wert thou my enemy, O thou my friend,
> How wouldst thou worse, I wonder, than thou dost
> Defeat, thwart me?

But why does God withdraw, hide himself, desert his faithful? To ask this is to enter the questioning phase of the experience. In "Carrion Comfort," Hopkins asks:

> But ah, but O thou terrible, why wouldst thou rude on me
> Thy wring-world right foot rock? lay a lionlimb against me? scan
> With darksome devouring eyes my bruised bones? and fan,
> O in turns of tempest, me heaped there; me frantic to avoid thee
>   and flee?
>
> (Poems, no. 64)

And if there is purpose in the trial, who is cheered by it? That too is in doubt. Recalling his own conversion, Hopkins goes on to ask:

Cheer whom though? The hero whose heaven-handling flung me,
    foot trod
Me? or me that fought him? O which one? is it each one?
    That night, that year
Of now done darkness I wretch lay wrestling with (my God!)
    my God.

As an emergent supplication to which this experience gives rise, the following, though early, is illustrative:

Oh! till Thou givest that sense beyond,
To shew Thee that Thou art, and near,
Let patience with her chastening wand
Dispel the doubt and dry the tear;
And lead me child-like by the hand
If still in darkness not in fear.

Speak! whisper to my watching heart.
                ("Nondum")

And I have already quoted Hopkins's basic supplication, "send my roots rain."

Hopkins never denies there is purpose in the encagement and desolation. And there is acceptance also. But for these, man must await the third act, the act of grace.

Isolation from God brings with it, or is preceded by it (probably it works both ways), isolation from other people as well. This might be a felt isolation from other specific known individuals with whom one has had, or could have, a close relationship. It might be an isolation from other specific unknown individuals as well, that is, other persons. Or it might be a sense of alienation from humanity or mankind in general.

The particular contexts and kinds of isolation will be different for different people undergoing the experience of encagement and desolation. Hopkins's own specific isolations are mainly of bio-graphical interest. But there are several passages of great importance for a general phenomenology of isolation. One of these suggests that there is a primordial feeling of estrangement underlying the specific isolations one may feel. In Hopkins's words: "To seem the stranger lies my lot, my life/Among strangers." This is probably a feeling that many people have felt—a sense of estrangement, distance, and alienation from humanity, even if there is no immediate specific object that dominates the feeling. One feels apart from mankind; all people seem strangers, and one feels oneself a stranger in the world. This feeling is probably universal in all isolation that is related to the experience of encagement, though it may not always predominate inasmuch as specific isolations can easily absorb one's attention. The suggestion is, in short, that felt desertion by God and felt estrangement from humanity are interrelated.

As illustrations of specific isolations, one may cite Hopkins's own estrangements from his family and from his homeland. Following the "stranger" line just quoted, he says:

> ... Father and mother dear,
> Brothers and sisters are in Christ not near
> And he my peace/my parting, sword and strife.

Alienation from England is then expressed in this late poem as well, but was also declared earlier in "The Loss of the Eurydice":

> Day and night I deplore
> My people and born own nation,
> Fast foundering own generation.
> (*Poems*, no. 41, st. 22)

One can also feel isolation from other individuals whom one does not know. An illustration of this occurs in "The Lantern out of Doors." The poem is prompted by the experience of seeing unknown persons going past at night with their lanterns. Hopkins is led to reflect:

> Men go by me whom either beauty bright
> In mould or mind or what not else makes rare:
> . . . .
> Death or distance soon consumes them: wind
> What most I may eye after, but in at the end
> I cannot, and out of sight is out of mind.
> (*Poems*, no. 40)

Of course it might be said that this experience is inevitable, and nothing unusual, in view of the vast numbers of persons one cannot know individually. Still there may be a difference between a sense of solidarity and a feeling of estrangement as one moves silently among these unknown people.

What is it that makes this isolation possible, whether it be the general estrangement from humanity or the more specific isolations felt by any given individual? Why are we subject to isolation from others? In Hopkins, there can be but one answer: the fallen condition of man. If all men were living in a perfect original state of creation and grace, there would be a beautiful accord of man with God and of people among themselves; there would be, in the modern phrase, a genuine community among persons. But man's sinful state has spoiled this ideal and rendered isolation frequent. Hopkins's awareness of man's fallen condition is vented in "The Sea and the Skylark." Man is compared with these two creations in nature:

> How these two shame this shallow and frail town!
>   How ring right out our sordid turbid time,
> Being pure! We, life's pride and cared-for crown,
>   Have lost that cheer and charm of earth's past prime:
> Our make and making break, are breaking, down
>   To man's last dust, drain fast towards man's first slime.
>   (*Poems*, no. 35)

"On the Portrait of Two Beautiful Young People" ends with the following lines:

> O but I bear my burning witness though
> Against the wild and wanton work of men.
>   (*Poems*, no. 157)

So a sense of man's degraded condition is likely to accompany the feeling of isolation since it is the condition preventing the communion with others.

4.   The Existential Climax

All of these elements of the experience may combine and eventually swell into a universal, cosmic sorrow, a Weltschmerz. One may come to lament existence itself and all finite beings driven by the flux of existence.

Hopkins uses the term "world-sorrow" explicitly on one occasion in "No worst, there is none" and utters a heartrending cry of its reality and power:

> My cries heave, herds-long; huddle in a main, a chief-
>   woe, world-sorrow; on an age-old anvil wince and sing—
> Then lull, then leave off. Fury had shrieked 'No ling-
>   ering! Let me be fell: force I must be brief'.

It is as if all of the other sorrows, of entrapment and emptiness, of desertion and isolation, swell up into this all-consuming, this all-pervasive, this ultimate sorrow. One's personal encagement is felt as a part of the world's encagement, his personal desolation as but an instance of a universal desolation. Thus world-sorrow is, phenomenologically, the "chief-woe," and, ontologically, the ground of mankind's and one's own miserable lot.

> And still th'abysses infinite
> Surround the peak from which we gaze.
> Deep calls to deep, and blackest night
> Giddies the soul with blinding daze
> That dares to cast its searching sight
> On being's dread and vacant maze.
>   ("Nondum")

A transition to this world-sorrow might well be the mourning for nature's lot due to the spoliation of it by sinful human hands. Although "The world is charged with the grandeur of God," nevertheless

> Generations have trod, have trod, have trod;
> And all is seared with trade; bleared, smeared with toil;
> And wears man's smudge and shares man's smell: the soil
> Is bare now, nor can foot feel, being shod.
>   ("God's Grandeur")

One may see nature hacked to pieces right around one, as in the case of the poplars commemorated in "Binsey Poplars." This poem is devoted entirely to man's ruination of nature, declaring:

O if we but knew what we do
When we delve or hew—
. . . .
Where we, even where we mean
To mend her we end her.
(*Poems*, no. 43)

A more brooding, pathetic comment on nature, and one which suggests that beauty itself is tainted with sadness, can be found in the opening lines of "On the Portrait of Two Beautiful Young People":

O I admire and sorrow! The heart's eye grieves
Discovering you, dark tramplers, tyrant years.
A juice rides rich through bluebells, in vince leaves,
And beauty's dearest veriest vein is tears.

Ultimately, however, the object of world-sorrow is not nature's spoliation but existence itself. And ultimately the source of world-sorrow is not man's wantonness but the ruthless destructiveness of time itself, a wider ravaging in which even man is caught up.

More specifically, the objective conditions or sources of world-sorrow appear to be transitoriness and death. On the one hand, temporal passage means that all achievements, all good things, all perfections, must change, must be short-lived, must vanish. On the other hand, personal death is the quenching, the closing off of those particular efforts, hopes, goods everyone has known. All reduces to nought in death. Death and transitoriness are not, of course, unrelated. The inevitability of death is a personally felt consequence of the universal change wrought on all things by transitoriness.

The telling time our task is; time's some part,
Not all, but we were framed to fail and die.
("To His Watch," *Poems*, no. 153)

Heraclitus is the father of the conception of universal flux, and Hopkins's chief poem on this theme is entitled, "That Nature is a Heraclitean Fire and of the Comfort of the Resurrection." In it he first notes how weather right around us can lay waste earth's bounty, and then he declares that man himself is consumed by nature. The central passage is:

> ... Million-fueled, nature's bonfire burns on.
> But quench her bonniest, dearest to her, her clearest-selved spark
> Man, how fast his firedint, his mark on mind, is gone!
> Both are in an unfathomable, all is in an enormous dark
> Drowned. O pity and indignation! Manshape, that shone
> Sheer off, disseveral, a star, death blots black out; nor mark
>   Is any of him at all so stark
> But vastness blurs and time beats level.
>
> (*Poems*, no. 72)

In "The Wreck of the Deutschland" the transitoriness of life is compared with the sand slipping inevitably through an hourglass in stanza four:

>   I am soft sift
>   In an hourglass—at the wall
>   Fast, but mined with a motion, a drift,
>   And it crowds and it combs to the fall.

Our lot quickly runs out and is but a moment in the fall of time.

In "The Leaden Echo," the inevitability of death is sounded, and with it the destruction of beauty and vigor. First the chorus asks whether there is any way to keep beauty from vanishing. Then the answer comes echoing in response:

> No there's none, there's none, O no there's none,
> Nor can you long be, what you now are, called fair,
> Do what you may do, what, do what you may,
> . . . .
> ... no, nothing can be done
> To keep at bay
> Age and age's evils, hoar hair,
> Ruck and wrinkle, drooping, dying, death's worst, winding sheets,
>   tombs and worms and tumbling to decay.

In an early fragmentary poem, "I am like a slip of comet," one's hurdling toward death is coupled with a sense of his puniness in the cosmos.

—I am like a slip of comet,
Scarce worth discovery, in some corner seen
Bridging the slender difference of two stars,
(*Poems*, no. 103)

and, like the comet that is seen streaking through the universe and then disappearing,

So I go out: my little sweet is done:
I have drawn heat from this contagious sun:
To not ungentle death now forth I run.

Finally, the exquisite poem, "Spring and Fall," startlingly simple (for Hopkins) and yet movingly pathetic, captures in one stroke the transitoriness of nature, the inevitability of death, and the surrounding sense of somber, secluded sadness. A child is mourning the falling of golden leaves, but what she is really mourning is nature's mortality and her own eventual death. The poem declares that "sorrow's springs are the same," namely, death, and concludes:

It is the blight man was born for,
It is Margaret you mourn for.
(*Poems*, no. 55)

World-sorrow rooted in transitoriness and death, then, is the climactic outer penumbra of the experience of desolation.

If world-sorrow is the outwardly pointing climax of particular objects of sorrow, mental torture is the inwardly pointing climax of pain in the experience. The person undergoing the experience feels a terrific torment within, an acute mental suffering akin to acute bodily pain. The various elements of the experience crush the mind's well-being and bring an excruciating torture to the self.

There are three waves in this mental torment. The first is the wave of pure pain, that suffering which in the mental sphere is called agony. The second is anguish, which is agony mixed with and centered in a gnawing uncertainty in the self. The third is self-hatred, in which the person comes to despise and revile himself.

All of these themes can be illustrated from Hopkins. The selections this time come entirely from five of the desolation poems of his last years.[9] First, there is pure agony:

its pangs—

> No worst, there is none. Pitched past pitch of grief,
> More pangs will, schooled at forepangs, wilder wring.

its grating—

> We hear out hearts grate on themselves: it kills
> To bruise them dearer.

its grinding—

> shelterless, thoughts
> against thoughts in groans grind.

and its sheer torment—

> My own heart let me more have pity on; let
> Me live to my sad self hereafter kind,
> Charitable; not live this tormented mind
> With this tormented mind tormenting yet.

Agony continues in anguish, which adds the dread of uncertainty:

the uncertainty of fearfulness—

> O the mind, mind has mountains; cliffs of fall
> Frightful, sheer, no-man-fathomed. Hold them cheap
> May who ne'er hung there.

the uncertainty of darkness without direction or surcease—

> What hours, O what black hours we have spent
> This night! what sights you, heart, saw; ways you went!
> And more must, in yet longer light's delay.
> With witness I speak this. But where I say
> Hours I mean years, mean life.

and the uncertainty of comfortlessness—

> I cast for comfort I can no more get
> By groping round my comfortless, than blind
> Eyes in their dark can day or thirst can find
> Thirst's all-in-all in all a world of wet.

The burden of all this defeat, abandonment, sorrow, and torment may end in a bitter self-hate and self-scourging:

> I am gall, I am heartburn. God's most deep decree
> Bitter would have me taste: my taste was me;
> Bones built in me, flesh filled, blood brimmed the curse.
> .... I see
> The lost are like this, and their scourge to be
> As I am mine, their sweating selves; but worse.

*

Conclusion

One cannot say that everyone who undergoes encagement and desolation will experience exactly all of these elements with the same accents and prominences. Entrapment, nonfulfillment, and emptiness; disappointment, discouragement, and despair; desertion by God and isolation from others; world-sorrow; mental agony, anguish, and self-hate—these are probably like the traits appearing in a family relationship, where a certain set of traits characterizes the family as a whole while the specific traits occur in the individual family members in different patterns of dominance and recessiveness. Peter may be plagued more by a feeling of emptiness, James by isolation from others, John by world-sorrow. What one can say, however, is that these traits appear in Hopkins's poetic expression of encagement and desolation, and that this set of traits defines a mode of experience which many people seeking a spiritual life have encountered in some pattern or other.

So far I have only sounded the low notes in the total experience. There is more; there is resolution; there is life out of death. I said before in the section on desertion that the experience is a religious experience because it is related through and through to God. Now a further dimension of, and reason for, its religious character is on the horizon: the possibility of overcoming such pain. Nature and grace can provide a conquest, or partial conquest, over encagement's captivity and sorrow.

CHAPTER *III*

Naturation

IF HOPKINS'S poetry is, from one perspective, replete as a literature of encagement, it is no less replete as a literature of spiritual triumph. The distinctive character of this poetry, as compared with secular cries of despair, is that the reader is simultaneously caught up in the victory over encagement. Even as one is plunged, empathically, into the entrapment and desolation so powerfully portrayed, he is raised to the ridges of resolution. Thus the reader is convinced that where there is entrapment, there is release; where there is the threat of nonfulfillment, there is assurance of the success that alone matters; where there is emptiness, there is new birth; where there is despair, there is rejuvenation; where there is God's desertion, there is also God's steadfastness; where there is isolation from others, there is also communion; where there is world-sorrow, there is world-affirmation; where there is agony, there is also joy.

For Hopkins, these resolutions are not merely psychological states or emotional shifts. They are thoroughly religious, in the sense that they involve the individual's acceptance by, and acceptance of, and love of, and being loved by, the one eternal God. Nor should anyone think of these resolutions as automatically and totally replacing, eliminating, the harrowing elements of encagement. One may remain, to some extent, in these humanly persisting limitations—as Hopkins apparently did—to the end of life. It is the nature of this spiritual experience, and the triumph contained in it, that the resolutions may be locked with the problems in a living tension and

49

may conquer them in ongoing combat that may be as long as life itself. The encagement is real; but the release is more profound. The despair is real; but rejuvenation is possible. The torture is real; but there is solace.

The way of resolution begins with some steps that man can take through his own autonomy. It culminates in God's initiative on man's behalf. Of course, all is made possible by divine grace in the first place. But aside from this ultimate cause, this formal twofold distinction remains within the present life of man. The twofold division corresponds to a long-standing distinction in Christian tradition between nature and grace, which distinction Hopkins accepts, though as a Scotist he may not stress the degree of rational autonomy of a Thomist. In this regard, Hopkins's Catholic tradition differs from that of those Protestant movements which accentuate man's depravity and total appeal to grace.

This chapter considers the first of these emphases, which will be called naturation. What is it that man can do to help alleviate the devastation of spiritual dryness and desolation? What steps can he take that fall within his own effort?

1. *Openness to Beauty*

One profound thing a person can do is be open to beauty. Beauty is a powerful solvent to the corrosion of desolation. It seems fitting to begin consideration of naturation with this theme because of Hopkins's own intense absorption in beauty. It is not that the other steps of naturation to be met later are less significant, but rather that, as a poet in contrast to a moralist or theologian, Hopkins is more replete with the theme of beauty.

How can beauty, one may ask immediately, serve as a solvent? What can beauty do for the person desolate and in the grips of encagement?

One answer to this question is that beauty can strikingly alter one's attention, so that one becomes preoccupied not with self-absorption but with something outwardly magnificent. For example:

> ... thrush
> Through the echoing timber does so rinse and wring

> The ear, it strikes like lightnings to hear him sing.
> ("Spring," *Poems*, no. 33)

This shift in mood and interest may be temporary; but such breaks are helpful in cutting the intensity of despair and in reeducating habits of attention.

Hopkins addresses the question of beauty's role directly in "To What Serves Mortal Beauty?" He first poses the question in his own extended poetic way, and then gives a succinct two-part answer:

> To what serves mortal beauty—dangerous; does set danc-
>   ing blood—the O-seal-that-so feature, flung prouder form
> Than Purcell tune lets tread to? See: it does this: keeps warm
> Men's wits to the things that are; what good means.
>   (*Poems*, no. 62)

The last line contains the two-part answer. Beauty first opens one up "to the things that are." It would be possible to interpret these words in a rather psychological way by saying that beauty brings one sharply back to reality, whereas the depression experienced in encagement might have caused him to drift off into illusion and be cut off from reality. But this interpretation would be a bit of projected anachronism. As a Scotist, Hopkins is probably thinking of the inner form and meaning of each thing made especially manifest through the outward beauty people behold. To grasp the unique forms of things—their inscapes—is to be brought into the rich detail and power of individual beings which together constitute natural reality, and this absorption in individual things through their beauty is an exhilarating and healing experience.

The other part of the answer here is that beauty keeps man warm to "what good means." In a state of spiritual deprivation, one is likely to lose his focus on the good, on cherished ideals, on the way he should go. Beauty, by drawing the viewer into the forms of individual things, draws him also to the good, which is simply the perfection of each thing's being. There appears to be a multiple influence at work in this result. On the one hand, since beauty, as sensuous harmony, and good, as perfection of being, are universal and interrelated metaphysically, beauty can actually draw men toward the good of things and their own good. At the same time, it can remind anyone of the goodness in all creation and in himself and of his need to pursue that good. Then too—and this may be the most immediately felt influence—beauty may be a powerful and refreshing stimulus, kindling one's mental fires once again for the continuous struggle for goodness.

But there is more that beauty does as well. Not only can it draw one to the good, but it can enliven in a certain way his moral responsibility. In particular, it can arouse one's obligation to natural things and thereby to human beings served by natural things. This point is made several times in Hopkins's reflection on striking scenery. The underlying theme is that beauty in nature, not being conscious, is dependent upon man for its preservation. If this is so, and if one is captivated by beauty, one may in turn be aroused in one's responsibility. This sense of responsibility can also be restorative for a desolate mind.

The dependence of nature's beauty upon man is the central theme in "Ribblesdale":

> Earth, sweet Earth, sweet landscape, with leaves throng
> And louched low grass, heaven that dost appeal
> To, with no tongue to plead, no heart to feel;
> That canst but only be,...
> . . . .
> And what is Earth's eye, tongue, or heart else, where
> Else, but in dear and dogged man?
>
> (*Poems*, no. 58)

But man, "selfbent so bound, so tied to his turn," often acts with destruction, havoc, unconcern. Sometimes it seems as if he "gives all to rack or wrong." And this is why earth, despite its potential beauty, also wears "brows of such care, care and deep concern."

The destructiveness of man is movingly depicted in "Binsey Poplars." So thorough may be man's havoc that "After-comers cannot guess the beauty been."

But for any person who is captivated by the love of beauty and is devoted to it, his "selfbent" will may be turned to moral responsibility, and this will portend good not only for nature but for man himself whose natural life is so bound up with nature. And more, this responsibility brings a person closer to his fulfillment as a human being.

Finally, in asking what beauty can do, no one should ignore the simplest answer of all—that it can bring pure bliss and ecstasy to the psyche. The poems are rich in concrete descriptions of beauty; but amid these, there are occasional soundings of this ecstatic response. In "The Windhover," the ecstasy of a bird itself in its figure-skating around the sky evokes a similar feeling in the poet:

> ... My heart in hiding
> Stirred for a bird,—the achieve of, the mastery of the thing!
> Brute beauty and valour and act.

And in "Hurrahing in Harvest," whose very title indicates the mood in question, the reader is told that in the presence of beauty,

> The heart rears wings bold and bolder
> And hurls for him, O half hurls earth for him off under his feet.
> (Poems, no. 38)

What beauty does for man, then, in his state of spiritual dryness, may be summarized as follows:

1. It dramatically alters attention.
2. It makes him open to existing things.
3. It draws him to the goodness of being.
4. It sparks moral responsibility.
5. It brings ecstatic emotion.

No wonder Hopkins calls repeatedly for the preservation of natural beauty and natural environment, as in "Inversnaid": "Long live the weeds and the wilderness yet" (*Poems*, no. 56).

Hopkins's view of the function of beauty seems not unrelated to his conception of the status of beauty in reality. This conception may be summed up by saying that, for Hopkins, beauty is objective and universal. It is objective inasmuch as it pertains to things themselves: it is a characteristic of *them* and not simply of the mind. In "Hurrahing in Harvest," Hopkins says, after speaking of the "lovely behaviour" and "glory" and "majestic" quality of nature, that "These things, these things were here and but the beholder/ Wanting." And it is universal inasmuch as it pervades the entire creation.

> What is all this juice and all this joy?
> A strain of the earth's sweet being in the beginning.
> ("Spring")

The thought is also found in "The May Magnificat," where the poet refers to "that world of good" and "Spring's universal bliss," and concludes by speaking of "This ecstasy all through mothering earth" (*Poems*, no. 42).

If beauty is in things themselves and not just manufactured subjectively, then it has a power of its own to meet man in his encounter with it and stir an internal ecstasy. And if it is pervasive throughout the earth, then the opportunity for encountering it wherever one may be is immeasurably heightened. Thus the therapeutic power of beauty is grounded in reality.

Yet the rapture in beauty which the poems reveal is not sentimental. Nor is it unqualified or undiscriminating. Hopkins can speak of beauty as dangerous despite its delight, or perhaps because of it. The danger is that of distraction, deflection, false lure, when viewed from a total spirituality. This theme, intimated in "To What Serves Mortal Beauty?" is developed further in a letter of Hopkins to Bridges.[1]

The antidote to this danger is to see clearly that beauty is a mortal phenomenon, serving the good of naturation, but limited to that realm. Then no one will be persuaded to raise it to a false religion or to make it an all-consuming devotion. Natural beauty, Hopkins insists in "To What Serves Mortal Beauty?" is not an end in itself; it serves a higher purpose and focuses on a higher spiritual gift, that of grace. Meet beauty, yes; but having met it, " then leave, let that alone./Yea, wish that though, wish all, God's better beauty, grace." Natural beauty must recognize grace as a better beauty, and it should be dedicated to the source of that grace:

> This, all this beauty blooming,
> This, all this freshness fuming,
> Give God while worth consuming.
> ("Morning, Midday, and Evening Sacrifice," *Poems,* no. 49)

Thus seen in perspective, beauty's danger is neutralized and its therapy in naturation freed.

How, then, one might ask, can beauty, with its healing quality, be possessed? Can it be harnessed? Today's world might think that it could be "engineered" for its great utility. Not so, Hopkins says, in effect, in "To What Serves Mortal Beauty?" It can only be approached and accepted: "What do then? how meet beauty? Merely meet it; own,/Home at heart, heaven's sweet gift."

This openness to beauty permits one then to find beauty, and with it a natural restoration, just about anywhere in nature. Numerous and variegated are the things in nature which intrigue Hopkins in this regard throughout his poetry. They include seasons and their special features, landscapes and furrowed fields, trees and birds, stars and sun, clouds and wind, brooks and streams, grass and earth, flowers and fruits, and more. And not to be omitted is the human form itself, the "beauty of body" celebrated in "Harry Ploughman."

Thus beauty, in its myriads of individual forms, can help break the bonds of encagement, though it has the limitations of all natural means and must eventually yield priority. Meanwhile, there are other means of naturation.

2.   The Role of Activity

Openness to beauty is essentially contemplation. But activity is no less a naturation. Here one encounters the historic contrast between contemplation and activity, sometimes said to compose the unity of man, sometimes the source of tension in human life, sometimes the difference between the Greeks and the moderns, the East and the West, and so on. From the present perspective, one can see both as antidotal to despair in Hopkins's thought. This study will consider three kinds of human activity—creative expression, moral endeavor, and daily work.

For Hopkins himself, creative expression took the form of art, chiefly poetry, but did not exclude music and painting.[2] For others, creative expression would be different and would be related to their unique beings as individual persons.

The Scotist emphasis on individuality of form gives a foundation for believing in the possibility of self-expression and its beneficent effect. Each being has its own selfhood to express. In the metaphysical poem, "As Kingfishers Catch Fire," Hopkins accents this Scotist doctrine:

> Each mortal thing does one thing and the same:
> Deals out that being indoors each one dwells;
> Selves—goes itself; *myself* it speaks and spells,
> Crying *What I do is me: for that I came.*
>
> *(Poems*, no. 57)

The poem deserves further attention in connection with a study of the Scotist doctrine itself.[3] For now, only its relevance to naturation is noted: its supplying of the ground for believing in the possibility of healing creativeness.

Many are the kinds of creative expression, as I have already said. But Hopkins's interest was artistic work; I would like to return to that subject now.

What he seems to admire most in artistic work, as indicated in "Henry Purcell," is the way in which an artist reveals his own individuality, his own peculiar genius. In doing this, an artist can illumine each man's individuality and in this sense speak for the unique being and worth of every person. Purcell has not merely "given utterance to the moods of man's mind, he has, beyond that, uttered in notes the very make and species of man as created both in him and in all men generally."[4]

> Not mood in him nor meaning, proud fire or sacred fear,
> Or love or pity or all that sweet notes not his might nursle:
> It is the forged feature finds me; it is the rehearsal
> Of own, of abrupt self there so thrusts on, so throngs the ear.
>
> *(Poems*, no. 45)

The artistic act, then, either engaged in directly or experienced vicariously through another, can reach the true self and lift it out of the pit of despair: "Let him oh! with his air of angels then lift me."

Another palliative characteristic of artistic expression is its sense of abandon. In artistic creation can come a restoration of inner psychical freedom that has been trampled underground by the tractor of depression. I believe "The Windhover" illustrates this, though the bird also symbolizes Christ. The two themes are not, after all, unrelated: Christ shows a perfect spiritual freedom despite his presence in natural limitations and sufferings. The windhover, circling and swooping in the air, shows the abandon, the gracefulness, the pure movement that is possible to a free spirit. Like the "striding high there" of the falcon, "the hurl and gliding" of artistic expression can "rebuff" the resistance of encagement.

But can it be accomplished? It would seem there is a vicious paradox: artistic expression can palliate depression, but the very depression may be what is preventing artistic expression. Hopkins certainly testifies to the latter, as is seen in both his poems and his letters. But he also testifies to the former. In "The Caged Skylark," which we took as the *locus poeticus* of encagement, he can say, of both caged bird and bound man: "Both sing sometimes the sweetest, sweetest spells."

How then is this possible? The answer must be the nature of man. Within the essence of the individual there is the potentiality, the deep resource, for imaginative breakthrough.

The process may involve as much patience as activity. This idea can surely be read as one meaning behind the account of the creative act in Hopkins's last poem, "To R.B." That is, one's life itself, like the poetic mind, may need to wait in brooding.

> The fine delight that fathers thought; the strong
> Spur, live and lancing like the blowpipe flame,
> Breathes once and, quenched faster than it came,
> Leaves yet the mind a mother of immortal song.
> Nine months she then, nay years, nine years she long
> Within her wears, bears, cares and combs the same.

Yet, despite the waiting and the discouragement over loss of inspiration, creative expression can break through, if only to utter the discouragement. This in fact was Hopkins's triumph in his last years: though weighted with desolateness, he could nonetheless express that state in the deepest, deepest swells.

Another activity available for combating the deteriorating effects of encagement is moral resolution and action. The capacity of will, like the capacity for creative expression, remains ever a potential power on which man can draw. Certainly the moral life is bound to be enervated with respect to its usual motives and sanctions. But moral resolve can always continue at some level. Perhaps it may seem as if one can do almost nothing any more; but one can do *something* at least. "I can," Hopkins affirms in "Carrion Comfort," "Can something, hope, wish day come, not choose not to be." One begins where one is in the state of desolation and makes whatever immediate resolves are relevant: one can at least hope for relief; one can at least wish that this night, in which despair is often most acute, will pass into another day; one can at least refrain from giving up one's being deliberately. Further resolutions and wider endeavors may then become possible.

That this is indeed a resource for man, open to his power of choice, is part of the natural law tradition in Christianity which Hopkins accepts. There are several allusions to this fundamental belief in his poetry. Here is one from "The Times are Nightfall":

> ... There is your world within.
> There rid the dragons, root out there the sin.
> Your will is law in that small commonweal.

All human capacities are, of course, part of man's original creation by divine act. But they then become open to natural employment. One can always, therefore, despite the deepest despair, turn to the inner self at least, even though outward paths may be blocked, to persist in duty and in moral resolution. The natural light within can hold one in a steady course.

> What the heart is! which, like carriers let fly—
> Doff darkness, homing nature knows the rest—
> To its own fine function, wild and self-instressed.
> ("The Handsome Heart," *Poems*, no. 47)

With this foundational conviction about man's moral nature, it is possible to appraise oneself meaningfully, to chastise oneself, and to exhort oneself to take the measures available to counteract desolation. And in fact one does find such exhorations in Hopkins. The last quotation but one includes one of these. Here is another from "The Candle Indoors":

> Come you indoors, come home; your fading fire
> Mend first and vital candle in close heart's vault:
> You there are master, do your own desire.

Even in the midst of a desolation poem, "My own heart let me more have pity on," in which the poet speaks of his "tormented mind," he can exhort himself:

> Soul, self; come, poor Jackself, I do advise
> You, jaded, let be; call off thoughts awhile
> Elsewhere; leave comfort root-room.
>
> (*Poems*, no. 69)

The outward moral life also is not ignored, although in a state of desolation it may appear dimmed because the inner moral resolve may seem to be the only thing left in life, and even this in a very weakened condition. But the injunctions to protect natural surroundings in "Ribblesdale," and the injunction "Each be other's comfort kind" in "The Wedding March," are examples clearly indicating that the totality of the moral outlook is being preserved. National service can also be an outward form of moral resolve for Hopkins. An unfinished poem with a chorus begins:

> What shall I do for the land that bred me,
> Her homes and fields that folded and fed me?
> Be under her banner and live for her honour.
>
> (*Poems*, no. 156)

And duties in society are open: in "Tom's Garland," it is suggested that one can be concerned "if all had bread;" one can work "in wide the world's weal;" one can "care, but share care" (*Poems*, no. 70).

In the end, one may come to interpret the state of desolation, for all its predominance of emptiness and despair, as having a profound moral function. This function is that of jolting everyone, in the sharpest, most direct, most undiluted form possible, into a confrontation with right and wrong and the demand to decide for the right. The haunting and mysterious throes of "Spelt from Sibyl's Leaves" culminates in this thought. The night of torture and self-examination descends, and in this blackness "all the sensuous delight in appearances, as well as all the half-truths and ambiguities with which we surround ourselves in life—are swallowed up, and nothing but absolute right and wrong remains."[5]

> ... Let life, waned,
>   ah let life wind
> Off her once skeined stained veined variety upon, all on two
>   spools; part, pen, pack
> Now her all in two flocks, two folds—black, white; right,
>   wrong; reckon but, reck but, mind
> But these two; ware of a world where but these two tell, each
>   off the other.

And so, in another of those paradoxes of religious experience, it may be that not only can moral resolve aid in conquering the desolation but the desolation may in fact be a vehicle through which the priority and purity of moral resolve are brought clearly before all men.

One of the most concrete and comprehensive outcomes of moral resolve is persistence in the vocation, the daily work, in which one is engaged. The ability to do one's daily tasks is likely to be an early casualty of a depressed spirit. And yet, if the work can be persisted in, which persistence is possible to moral effort, it can be a stalwart steadying resource. It can utilize and organize time instead of wasting it; it can deflect interest away from self-pity; it can keep alive a sense of constructive contribution. Hopkins's own life exemplifies this persistence in daily work despite overwhelming physical and mental hardships. His poems contain both allusions to the importance of work and actual celebrations of it.

The esteem in which work is held is shown by Hopkins's association of it with the coveted quality of inner peace, as in the poem entitled "Peace": "And when Peace here does house/He comes with work to do, he does not come to coo." And here is an example of what work can mean to a laborer, symbolized by Tom in "Tom's Garland":

> Tom Heart-at-ease,...
> ... Tom seldom sick,

> Seldomer heartsore; that treads through, prickproof, thick
> Thousands of thorns, thoughts.

To celebrate work is to affirm both the people who do the work and the particular work that they do. Both notes are struck in the poems.

Among the types of people depicted in their work by Hopkins are a ploughman, a miner, a farrier, a sailor, a soldier, an artist, a cleric. These are, of course, but poetic examples. Others would serve as well.

All workers, being human, are valued, of course, as creatures of worth and dignity. But in so far as they are seen as symbolic representatives of work, they are prized and praised specifically because of their calling.

> ... Here it is: the heart,
> Since, proud, it calls the calling manly, gives a guess
> That, hopes that, makesbelieve, the men must be no less;
> It fancies, feigns, deems, dears the artist after his art.
> ("The Soldier," *Poems,* no. 63)

The calling itself is cherished even if in practice the people, despite their human worth and dignity, may be "frail clay, nay but foul clay." Thus the inherent worth of man as a created being brings dignity to the work he does; and the work itself, because of its inherent potential for service and fulfillment, brings dignity to fallen man or, more particularly for the purpose of this study, troubled man. The person active in his work brings glory to God, and, more particularly for this purpose, finds thereby a measure of restoration for his troubled soul.

The best-known celebrations of created things, in Hopkins, are probably "God's Grandeur" and "Pied Beauty." The former alludes to the earth-smearing side effects of human trade and toil; but the latter exalts the trades themselves as human work. Glory is due to God, it says, for all natural things "And all trades, their gear and tackle and trim."

Daily work, then, like the activities of creative expression and moral endeavor, can also help to nourish the thirsty roots in people. It too is a natural rain against complete dryness. And so is human contact.

3.   *Human Association*

The value of human association as a natural healing power may never seem as real and momentous as during times of depression and sorrow. This recourse of recovery may be more stable and solid than other natural avenues because of its omnipresent potentiality. Beauty may be clouded by depression; creative expression may fail; moral resolve and spiritual discipline may falter; daily work may slacken; but human association has an ever-present potentiality for restorative power.

The restorative balm of human association may come through a wide range of degrees in human feeling, all the way from mere human contact—a limited natural grace in itself—to the depths of personal fellowship and love. Even in the slender corpus of poems that Hopkins was able to produce, one finds this range of feeling reflected. One also finds a wide variety of persons referred to in these expressions of human feeling. There are references to family and friends, to children, to the sick and the victims of accident, to strangers, to workers, to fellow believers, to religious supplicants, to past heroes, and to mankind as such.

The poem beginning "To seem the stranger" has a succinct statement of this power. This poem is especially timely since it illustrates what I said at the beginning of the chapter, namely, the paradoxical truth that encagement, here called the "third remove," is simultaneously embroiled with the means of recovery. Thus, even while lamenting alienation from dear ones and country, Hopkins can say:

> I am in Ireland now; now I am at a third
> Remove. Not but in all removes I can
> Kind love both give and get.

It is also clear from this poem that, despite denominational separation from family, they are still close to him.

One of the 1877 sonnets, "In the Valley of the Elwy," gives us, in purest simplicity, the feeling of warmth and affection received from hospitable friends:

> I remember a house where all were good
> To me, God knows, deserving no such thing.
>   (*Poems*, no. 34)

Affection can extend even to unknown strangers when one has an affirmative attitude toward the human community. In "The Lantern out of Doors," Hopkins evinces this human tie with unknowns and then laments the fact that finite life does not permit more than a momentary contact with most people one meets in passing. In "Cheery Beggar," the poet pauses to admire a man whose "heart is fine" and "whom want could not make pine" (*Poems*, no. 142). Regarding a country shepherd boy, an early fragment, "Fragments of Richard," muses upon his "gentle sense of fellowship" (*Poems*, no. 107).

Several of the poems reveal a special fondness for children. One of these already cited is "Spring and Fall." In "The Handsome Heart," a tender response is composed "at a gracious answer" given by a ten-year-old boy. The poem, "Brothers," captures with equal tenderness the feelings of a child at a children's play in which his brother is performing.

Sympathy with the sick and with the victims of accident is rendered in several poems. The two longest poems, the two "wreck" poems, unfold dramatically in response to the inexplicable way in which fellow creatures became caught up in natural disasters. A more personal account is found in "Felix Randal":

> This seeing the sick endears them to us, us too it endears.
> My tongue had taught thee comfort, touch had quenched thy tears;
> Thy tears that touched my heart, child, Felix, poor Felix Randal.
> (*Poems*, no. 53)

This poem and others like "Tom's Garland" and "Harry Ploughman" also illustrate sympathy with workers in their various trades and vocations.

Human feeling can also extend to companions of the past. Duns Scotus and Henry Purcell, for example, come in for special full-length tributes in Hopkins's poetry. Scotus is, to Hopkins, the one "who of all men most sways my spirits to peace." And of Purcell, Hopkins writes:

> Have fair fallen, O fair, fair have fallen, so dear
> To me, so arch-especial a spirit as heaves in Henry Purcell.

And of course there is comradeship celebrated in relation to fellow believers, fellow supplicants, fellow Catholics, which goes beyond mere denominational connection. Many of Hopkins's occasional religious pieces are of this sort and have a significance for that reason beyond their occasional character. A passage from "The Bugler's First Communion" is illustrative:

> A bugler boy from barrack (it is over the hill
> There)...
> . . . .
> Came, I say, this day to it—to a First Communion.
> . . . .
> How it does my heart good, visiting at that bleak hill,
> When limber liquid youth, that to all I teach
>   Yields tender as a pushed peach,
> Hies headstrong to its wellbeing of a self-wise self-will!
> . . . .
> Nothing else is like it, no, not all so strains
> Us: freshyouth fretted in a bloomfall all portending
>   That sweet's sweeter ending:
> Realm both Christ is heir to and there reigns.
>   (*Poems*, no. 48)

The balm of human feeling in times of despair is, phenomenologically viewed, natural, spontaneous, uncomplicated by thought and doctrine. Not that everyone can automatically be consoled by it, for internal inhibitions can block. But it has the potentiality of operating universally and naturally regardless of particular doctrinal belief or disbelief. Yet there is a theological basis for it within the Christian outlook that Hopkins avows. This basis is in the original created goodness and worthiness of man. Although Hopkins has much to say about the baseness and sinfulness of man, in keeping with Christian belief, he nevertheless also celebrates the original created worth of man. Of man he can say, in "To What Serves Mortal Beauty?";

> To man, that needs would worship block or barren stone,
> Our law says: Love what are love's worthiest, were all known;
> World's loveliest—men's selves.

If man is "love's worthiest," then if one associates and shares with this creature of worth, one too will be drawn into the worth and goodness that can overcome the encagement, loneliness, defiance, and agitation into which one has fallen. Each person, by being originally among "love's worthiest," can be potentially a balm to another. By association with the "world's loveliest—men's selves," one's own stature is renovated. A prescription for the disease of desolation then becomes: "Love what are love's worthiest... men's selves."

There is also an incarnational element in this view of human association and its potentiality. According to that doctrine, the vehicle for mediation between God and man is, after all, human embodiment. Using the idea of analogy (though not referring to theological salvation), one could then say that, pristinely, all persons are potentially mediating vehicles for the restoration of other persons within the times, places, and situations in which they find themselves. Just as Christ restores, each person can be a healing vehicle for another in time of trouble. In this way is the human community designed.

Of course one is dealing here with potentialities and not invariable actualities unrelated to freedom and folly. Still, human relatedness as an aspect of naturation is a real and grounded fact.

Perhaps I can go further and say not only that human association can be positively therapeutic but that the absence of human contact can be decisively destructive. There is a suggestion to this effect in a youthful poem, "A Vision of the Mermaids," which, along with some other poems, survived Hopkins's poem-burning of 1868. In this poem he is speaking of mermaids; but there is a symbolic reference to man.

> And a sweet sadness dwelt on everyone;
> I knew not why,—but know that sadness dwells
> On Mermaids—whether that they ring the knells
> Of seamen whelm'd in chasms of the mid-main,
> As poets sing; or that it is a pain
> To know the dusk depths of the ponderous sea,
> The miles profound of solid green, and be
> With loath'd cold fishes, far from man—or what;—
> I know the sadness but the cause know not.
>
> (*Poems*, no. 2)

Could it be that the most loathsome condition of human existence is to be devoid of human contact, to be "with loath'd cold fishes, far from man?" If so, how profound and significant is the realization of the opposite extreme, human solidarity and love, as intimated in this simple and prayerful meditation:

> But thou bidst, and just thou art,
> Me shew mercy from my heart
> Towards my brother, every other
> Man my mate and counterpart.
>   ("Thee, God, I come from," *Poems*, no. 155)

Now this study turns to the final stage of naturation.

4.   *Spiritual Discipline*

Regular spiritual exercises, and in general a constancy in spiritual discipline, are usually considered religious acts and not elements in naturation as here defined. Certainly their spiritual function is fittingly seen as their raison d'être. That is, they are directed toward the worship or revering of God himself; they may also be felt as a religious obligation per se; and they prepare the soul or personality for the reception of gifts of grace. Nevertheless, they may be viewed psychologically as well. They may have very real potential for therapeutic consequences. They may forestall waywardness of purpose, may fill a gnawing vacuum of time, may deflect the barrenness of brooding, and may even bring their own consolation and comfort. There are suggestions to this effect in some of Hopkins's poems.

One of the most straightforward places in which this intimation is given is "Carrion Comfort," in which, even though it is one of the dark desolation poems, Hopkins still finds space in two lines to reflect upon his decision to undertake the spiritual quest and to note the strength and joy it brought.

> Nay in all that toil, that coil, since (seems) I kissed the rod,
> Hand rather, my heart lo! lapped strength, stole joy, would
>   laugh, cheer.

Again, in "The Bugler's First Communion," he can speak of the consolation in teaching the faith and in administering the eucharist. In this spiritual work it is possible for one to "tread tufts of consolation days after."

There are numerous places where Hopkins enjoins to spiritual discipline without identifying any therapeutic byproducts. This is as it should be: they are not its aim. One may infer, however, by analogy with passages like the above, that similar benefits may accrue. In an early poem, "The Habit of Perfection," Hopkins urges that all of the body's members—lips, eyes, palate, nostrils, hands, etc.—be devoted to the life of Silence and Poverty. Of the later poems, lines like these are representative:

> Head, heart, hand, heel, and shoulder
> That beat and breathe in power—
> This pride of prime's enjoyment
> Take as for tool, not toy meant
> And hold at Christ's employment.
> ("Morning, Midday, and Evening Sacrifice")

In "The Starlight Night," one finds a more subtle suggestion: spiritual discipline may not only have beneficial consequences but may actually be indispensable for receiving the bounties that are in nature's store. The question is: what is the requirement for the boons of naturation? For example, this could mean: "What is the price of a true love and understanding of the beauty of the universe?"[6] For an answer, the relevant lines are:

> Ah well! it is all a purchase, all is a prize.
> Buy then! bid then!—What?—Prayer, patience, alms, vows.
> (*Poems*, no. 32)

The first line, which follows portrayals of the stars, suggests that there is a rich field of natural goodness to be harvested; but that in order to reap it, something is demanded of the beneficiary. It is bought at some cost to the individual. In the second line people are urged to pay the price but are reminded, perhaps with shock, that this payment may involve acts of spiritual discipline.

This concept surely reveals a deeper dimension of the relation between spiritual discipline and the overcoming of encagement. It also confirms that spiritual discipline is a part of naturation; for if spiritual discipline is necessary in order to reap the fullest measure of the harvest of natural goodness, then the implication is that there is something open to man, something he can accomplish spiritually, even within the realm of naturation short of grace.

In "The Golden Echo," a further and still more complex phase of this kind of naturation is presented. One must recognize, first of all, that there may be no obvious and direct therapeutic effects of spiritual discipline. Moreover, one also gives up something, forfeits some other good, in order to devote oneself wholeheartedly to the discipline. Here then is a paradox: not only may spiritual discipline bring no direct easement but it may actually involve forfeiture of other possible goods. Yet this situation is superseded by a higher paradox of hope and faith. The forfeiture, so the devotee is convinced, is being preserved in a more significant form and will be returned at the appropriate time and circumstance. One believes his true good is being nourished with a more profound care than he himself could have given it. One does not know when or where the realization of this good will effervesce; but one is assured in faith that it is being readied for accomplishment beyond his immediate knowledge. This assurance brings a contentment even amid natural desolation and perhaps the most profound contentment one can have. By this route, so complex in statement but so simple in act, the weariness of life is alleviated.

> O then, weary then why should we tread? O why are we so
>   haggard at the heart, so care-coiled, care-killed, so fagged,
>   so fashed, so cogged, so cumbered,
> When the thing we freely forfeit is kept with fonder a care,
> Fonder a care kept than we could have kept it, kept
> Far with fonder a care (and we, we should have lost it) finer,
>   fonder
> A care kept.—Where kept? do but tell us where kept, where.—
> Yonder.—What high as that! We follow, now we follow.—
>   Yonder, yes yonder, yonder,
> Yonder.

Thus the bonds of encagement, though not broken, are in a measure transcended in the convictions of hope and faith.

In summary, spiritual discipline can bring direct psychological aid in regard to, for example, psychic integration and time deployment. Secondly, it may even be essential for the attainment of certain natural goods. And thirdly, it may, through the necessary forfeiture of some goods and the anticipation of renewed attainments, foster the contentment of hope and faith. This is the human, therapeutic side of spiritual discipline, as contrasted with a divine, theological side.

Conclusion.

The means of naturation have not been exhausted here but some have been centered on as illustrative because they are prominent in Hopkins's poetry. Two others are worth mentioning in conclusion because they are prominent in Hopkins's own life. These are intellectual pursuits and good humor.

Reference to the intellect brings this study back from the more practical activities that it has been considering to something more like aesthetic contemplation. Intellectual pursuits are, of course, in one sense, activities. But their final aim, as Hopkins would agree, is not to be doing something but to know and enjoy the truth. Hopkins maintains the Aristotelian tradition that man is essentially a rational being, and thus reason's functioning is a fitting and proper part of his nature and a permanent potential in naturation. Hopkins's own life and letters illustrate how intellectual interests helped to keep him going through many a dark day. So one may certainly presume that scholarly persistence, or intellectual pursuits of any worthwhile kind, will have a central place in a phenomenology of naturation based on Hopkins. Intellectual endeavor, like beauty, has the deep power of keeping a person in a state of fascination and thereby enabling one to do what may be needed most during encagement, namely, to get outside himself. But it also has the capacity of sustaining this fascination in perpetuity. The life-long use of the mind, however long or short the life, is the resource spoken of here.

Good humor may seem to be of a different order, though it has a connection with intellect through wit. There are no humorous poems in the main corpus of Hopkins's 1876-89 poems. However, his letters display a striking wit. Also, the more than eighty incomplete poems in his work are presented in the fourth edition of the poems under the title, "UNFINISHED POEMS, FRAGMENTS, LIGHT VERSE &c."[7] So there is enough evidence to support the view that Hopkins valued wit and humor and regarded them as among the natural gifts of man. If they are, they too can enter the process of naturation. Maintaining a steady lighter side can enable one to look at one's own condition with some detachment and with less morose involvement. The fact is that though man weeps, he can also laugh; though he grieves, he can also be of good cheer. As an early fragment puts it:

> Laughing or tears. I think I could do either—
> So strangely elemented is my mind's weather,
> That tears and laughter are hung close together.
>   (Fragments of "Floris in Italy," *Poems*, no. 102)

Good humor, then, may pass into a more cheered and cheery condition, a cheerfulness toward life and even toward death. The following lines from the same poem point forward symbolically to Hopkins's own cheerful death despite his troublesome last years:

> It does amaze me, when the clicking hour
> Clings on the stroke of death, that I can smile.

Hopkins's own last words are reported to be: "I am so happy, so happy."[8]

Desolation gives way to life-restoring balm and good cheer through natural efforts. But the depiction of the process still awaits completion.

CHAPTER *IV*

Grace

NATURE AND grace—these are the two basic sources of response in human life—what each person can do for himself and what is done for him. Man can do much, but it is not given to him to do all. Hence what he can do by nature gives way to what he receives by grace. It is the grace-induced, grace-filled aspects of the experience studied here that now demand attention.

The total ENG experience—in abstract essence or model—is a movement from desolation to its opposite, consolation, a movement from the privations felt in consequence of encagement to the fullness of life characteristic of liberation. Despair yields to hoping and then joy; desertion reverts to returning and then homecoming; self-torment relents into recovering and then resilience. The intermediate cadences in the movement are partly effected by the original natural endowments with which man was created. The culmination of the experience, however, in so far as it is open to finite man, is felt as a deliverance effected from beyond oneself. It is attributed by the experient not to natural endeavor but to God's action. It is felt as a gift, a bestowal.

In such a way is the movement from desolation to consolation described in abstract essence. In actual practice, however, everyone knows that personal life is too precarious, too confused, too subject to ups and downs, for anyone to think that an abstract model is precisely duplicated on the slippery slope that is human life. I cannot say, then, that I am talking about exact chronological sequence.

The three stages of encagement, naturation, and grace represent a progression, yes; but it is a spiritual, vertical progression, not necessarily a chronological, horizontal sequence. It is not that encagement first stands all alone, then naturation takes the experient part way out of the ditch, then grace takes over to finish up. The various elements in these stages appear together in real life, give way to one another, intertwine and comingle in a varied, even crazy-quilt, manner. In particular, elements of naturation and of grace may be felt simultaneously, or one kind before the other, in the overcoming of encagement; and furthermore, there is no absolute guarantee against relapses into spiritual dryness.

Nevertheless, despite these real-life fluidities, it is convenient to view the experience as a three-stage progression in order to bring out the distinctive phenomenological elements in each phase. In such a way does one arrive at a bracketed study of grace in the experience, a phenomenology of grace.

The term "grace" in religion has the connotation of divine initiative rather than human effort. It is thus mainly a theological word. I include, therefore, the following theological definition of the concept of grace: "God's self-communication in his own divine life, both as given, and as accepted by man, is essentially God's free, personal, uncovenanted favor."[1] This definition gives the meaning of grace as a divine attribute manifested in a divine-human encounter. This study, on the other hand, has as its focus the ways in which grace is humanly felt and the vehicles through which it is mediated to man— a phenomenology rather than a theology of grace.

The elements of grace I shall cite are those indicated, of course, in the poetry of Hopkins. I cannot claim these as exhaustive, though I can claim them as fundamental. Before surveying these specific aspects of grace, I ought to suggest that, phenomenologically, the experience appears to have the following general characteristics: it is felt as originating from without, from beyond oneself; it is felt as flooding in and over one; it is felt as coming from a transcendent power; it is felt as unmerited, undeserved; it is felt as unexpected, a joyful surprise; it is felt with deep gratitude; it is felt as renewed strength; it is felt as resumed dedication. Now, this study turns to the modes of grace in Hopkins's poetry.

Grace, for Hopkins, appears first of all to be a source of enablement. It enables one to deal constructively with the distress, suffering, and evil of life, both practically and theoretically. It enables one then to renew one's calling and to see the entire world in new perspective. Beyond these enablements, one is then drawn into fuller spiritual progression. In religious idiom, fuller spiritual progression is growth in grace, or sanctification. In Christian context, it will consist mainly of an intensified sense of God's steadfastness and identification with Christ, pervaded by joy. These acts of enablement and acts of sanctification will each be considered in turn.

1.   Coping with Evil

The greatest threat of encagement, with its desolation, is complete enervation or nullification, the temptation to give in completely to the privation of one's being and the positive good one could attain. The temptation to give in is not to be thought of as the temptation to suicide. In fact, if one is talking about a *religious* experience throughout, with an underlying *faith* orientation, suicide will not be in the offing unless pathological disturbances creep in. Rather I am referring here to the temptation to yield to the tendencies at work in one's current situation to drift toward the annihilation of positive good. This destruction of positive good may take the form of mere vegetating and self-brooding, or it may involve overt actions that are not constructive.

With such an utter temptation in the offing, especially if it is actually yielded to in any measure, one is not likely to think of extrication from it as due to one's own moral ingenuity. The resistance to so dire an evil, and lesser evils that might come in its train, is attributed to rescue from beyond. The first experience of grace, then, is felt as a means of recovery from this primordial threat of privation. There must be, before anything else can be restored or accomplished, an elemental maintenance of the integrity of one's very being.

Hopkins begins his "Carrion Comfort" with a response to this elemental maintenance of being:

> Not, I'll not, carrion comfort, Despair, not feast on thee;
> Not untwist—slack they may be—these last strands of man
> In me or, most weary, cry *I can no more.* I can.

With the maintenance of one's being comes the strength to resist other, more specific evils and temptations. This is illustrated in a passage from "Felix Randal" which also illustrates another aspect of grace, namely, that it is often felt as being mediated through external acts, for example, the traditional "means of grace."

> Sickness broke him. Impatient, he cursed at first, but mended
> Being annointed and all; though a heavenlier heart began some
> Months earlier, since I had our sweet reprieve and ransom
> Tendered to him. Ah well, God rest him all road ever he
>   offended!

Besides this direct grace, felt either as rescue from complete disintegration or as the power to quell specific temptations, grace might be felt in the endowment of certain virtues that will enable a person then to resist evils himself as the occasion arises. These become instilled strengths to cope with evil. One of the virtues that Hopkins stresses in this regard is patience. There are references to it in several poems. In "Peace," after lamenting the absence of inner peace, he says:

> O surely, reaving Peace, my Lord should leave in lieu
> Some good! And so he does leave Patience exquisite,
> That plumes to Peace thereafter.

The poem devoted entirely to patience begins by saying that patience, though difficult, is nevertheless possible as a grace if sought: "Patience, hard thing! the hard thing but to pray,/But bid for, Patience is!" After indicating what patience requires, the poem then says what it can accomplish: it is "natural heart's ivy" that can mask the "ruins of wrecked past purpose." Moreover, when "our hearts grate on themselves" so that "it kills to bruise them dearer," we are still enabled to "bid God bend to him even so" our "rebellious wills." Patience is ivy against disintegration and temptation. Finally, because God himself is patient, we can receive the grace of patience through his activity:

> And where is he who more and more distills
> Delicious kindness?—He is patient. Patience fills
> His crisp combs, and that comes those ways we know.

If patience is a sturdy defense against temptations, love is a positive agent that will substitute for them. To receive the grace of love is the greatest gift. Hopkins speaks of this grace in "The Bugler's First Communion":

> O now well work that sealing sacred ointment!
> O for now charms, arms, what bans off bad
> And locks love ever in a lad!

This grace of love is the surest resistance in case one should "rankle and roam in backwheels though bound home."

With recovery from the extremity of the distraught state, with natural pursuits once again possible, one may even begin to see purposes at work in the trials one has undergone or is undergoing. This insight is part of the theoretical aspect of coping with evil. Of the formal problem of evil I shall have something to say in the chapter on the philosophy of religion.[2] Here I speak phenomenologically of the specific spiritual goods that the encaged one, now emerging, may come to see as attending his experience. Something significant, even stupendous, one might come to think, may be in process of accomplishment through it all.

What are some of these things being accomplished? The fundamental one, as far as the person's own change is concerned, is that of finding God anew. Another of the many paradoxes of religious experience is that suffering is sometimes a means to spiritual discovery. Desolation may thus be seen as having the function of shaking the individual into a realization of God's sovereignty and presence. Through the depths of despair one is prepared more fully to know and worship God. Hopkins expresses this paradox succinctly in the first stanza of "The Wreck of the Deutschland":

> Thou has bound bones and veins in me, fastened me flesh,
> And after it almost unmade, what with dread,
> Thy doing: and dost thou touch me afresh?
> Over again I feel thy finger and find thee.

This finding of God underlies all; but other subsidiary functions of encagement are also reported. I would like to cite and illustrate some of these further functions.

The experience may have the function of removing specific barriers to the knowing of God. Two of these barriers are mentioned in a single line in stanza six of "The Wreck of the Deutschland." They are guilt and hardheartedness. Guilt brings a sense of unworthiness and needs to be forgiven. Hardheartedness is a willful closing of oneself to others and needs to be broken down. One may come to feel that the stress of desolation is what was needed to overcome these barriers in oneself. Thus Hopkins can speak of such stress as something "That guilt is hushed by, hearts are flushed by and melt." To bring one into this greater openness is seen as divine intention in the desolation.

Divine intention is seen in all of the functions and is what is meant by purposes at work in encagement. For example, as another function, God may be seen as winnowing out our defects and purifying our spiritual being. Hopkins refers to this through the metaphor of chaff and grain. Why, then, do we suffer torment and tempest? "Why?" as he says in "Carrion Comfort": "That my chaff might fly; my grain lie, sheer and clear." And of the wrecking of the ship *Deutschland*, in particular, and of the tempest that caused the tragedy, Hopkins can nevertheless say in the end in stanza thirty-one: "is the shipwrack then a harvest,/does tempest carry the grain for thee?"

This study has already connected such tragedy to patience. That is, I mentioned earlier that the grace of patience is needed to face desolation. Now, in retrospect, the recovered one may see a function of desolation to be that of teaching this very patience. Certainly Hopkins connects the acquisition of patience with hardship and weariness:

> ... Patience who asks
> Wants war, wants wounds; weary his times, his tasks;
> To do without, take tosses, and obey.
>
> Rare patience roots in these, and, these away,
> Nowhere.
> ("Patience, hard thing!")

Desolation scourges us for patience.

More broadly, the desolation may be seen as getting man to turn away from the passing events of time and toward the eternal verities that endure. In "The Leaden Echo," it is intimated that the things of time, even the profound good of beauty, are passing and are therefore inherently a source of despair if they are all one has. But such a grim prospect directs him to the permanent good, so that he will, as "The Golden Echo" says,

> ...deliver it, early now, long before death
> Give beauty back, beauty, beauty, beauty, back to God,
>   beauty's self and beauty's giver.

To lead from the temporal to the eternal may be desolation's role.

Out of these experiences may come newly renovated selves forged as the crowning effect in man. This goal may be seen as the unifying function in the renewed person's life. Hopkins speaks of God's purpose here as that of making "new Nazareths in us" or "new Bethlehems," and continues:

> Bethlem or Nazareth,
> Men here may draw like breath
> More Christ and baffle death;
> Who, born so, comes to be
> New self and nobler me
> In each one.

("The Blessed Virgin compared to the Air we Breathe," *Poems,* no. 60)

Desolation's role is to help forge the new Christ-like selves each person was meant to be.

All of these functions mentioned so far—that of causing every man to find God, that of removing barriers to this end, that of clearing out each man's chaff, that of scourging him for patience, that of turning him to the eternal, that of leading him to his true self—may be seen as the inward, human consequences intended in the bitterness of encagement. They constitute the inwardly felt impact *upon* each one of us of divine purpose in the experience.

Yet there is one function that the devotee may come to uphold as overriding even all of these worthy ends. He may come to see the entire experience, suffered by him and by many another person, as a means whereby God is accomplishing his own will for mankind. This focus of function goes outward not inward. The fulfillment of God's will, then, is paramount, not merely the goods one may savor from it. The devotee merges with this purpose, as in the following plea of adoration from stanza ten of "The Wreck of the Deutschland":

> With an anvil-ding
> And with fire in him forge they will
> Or rather, rather then, stealing as Spring
> Through him, melt him but master him still:
> Whether at once, as once at a crash Paul,
> Or as Austin, a lingering-out sweet skill,
> Make mercy in all of us, out of us all
> Mastery, but be adored, but be adored King.

So enthralling may be this adoration of divine purpose that God is actually urged to accomplish his will through the wreck and storm of tribulation if that is what is needed. "Wring thy rebel," Hopkins beseeches in the previous stanza, "with wrecking and storm."

Nor is this a submission to mere might, sheer power, an arbitrary will, as is sometimes charged. And the reason it is not is that God's nature is, ultimately, love and mercy. So one is not merely succumbing to the arbitrariness of power but is opening out without reservation to the creative activity of love. In an audacious affirmation, Hopkins can write:

> I say that we are wound
> With mercy round and round
> As if with air.
> ("The Blessed Virgin Compared to the Air We Breathe")

The grace of felt divine purpose concludes, then, in a partnership of mercy.

2.   Outlook on Life and World

Being able to cope with evil and suffering, as an experienced form of grace, carries forward into life's activities and attitudes and is able to carry out a transforming effect thereupon. There are two phases here to consider: a sense of one's own calling and a new perspective on the larger world of human affairs and created things.

First of all, one may come to interpret one's work as motivated by, and hence exalted by, its being in the service of divine purpose. Believing in the worthwhileness of one's daily tasks is a major problem for many people, especially if those tasks appear routine, menial, or inconsequential. Even in jobs that call for imagination, adventure, and variety, spirits have been known to weaken and fade. Thus there is a need to see any job in wider perspective if it is to have persistent challenge and motivating worth. To have a sense of serving divine purpose provides such a perspective. It transforms daily tasks from a job into a vocation, from an occupation into a calling. One is able to see meaning in what one is doing here and now in the particular place and time into which one has been summoned. To have such a sense of calling is a priceless attribute to have in life, and yet it is really possible as Hopkins testifies in both poetry and life. And this priceless affection is indeed a grace from beyond oneself, as doubtless anyone can testify who has felt it, then felt it wane, then felt it return. Apart from grace, it would depend on the vagaries of job description, working conditions, incentive, mood, and the like, precarious things indeed for the continuity of a sense of mission. With a gracefilled sense of calling, a vocation can be meaningful and life steady, despite these natural and often wayward vagaries.

There is a beautiful example (and it is one of the few places in Hopkins's corpus where it seems appropriate to use the word "beautiful") of this sense of calling, inspired by grace, in a late poem of Hopkins honoring St. Alphonsus Rodriguez, a laybrother of the Jesuit society in Majorca. Alphonsus was a doorkeeper for forty years. By grace, he had inner victory and also outward purpose in his menial work. The poem begins by noting that one usually associates honor with great exploits and heroic deeds:

> Honour is flashed off exploit, so we say;
> And those strokes once that gashed flesh or galled shield
> Should tongue that time now, trumpet now that field,
> And, on the fighter, forge his glorious day.

There is a silent implication here that even such heroic laurels do not necessarily bring honor. On Christ, however, they do: "On Christ they do and on the martyr may." But heroic honor and acclaim are

not so forthcoming when the battle one faces is an inner, private
one (such as finding meaning in one's work):

> But be the war within, the brand we wield
> Unseen, the heroic breast not outward-steeled,
> Earth hears no hurtle then from fiercest fray.

Nevertheless, God is able to raise one's work to a higher calling and
to render the person honorable through his work:

> Yet God...
> . . . .
> Could crowd career with conquest while there went
> Those years and years by of world without event
> That in Majorca Alphonso watched the door.
>
> ("In Honour of St. Alphonsus Rodriguez," *Poems,* no. 73)

In "The Soldier," Hopkins intimates that callings can be blessed
in themselves and that their followers thus have a prima facie honor
just by virtue of such positions. The heart, he says,

> Since, proud, it calls the calling manly, gives a guess
> That, hopes that, makesbelieve, the men must be no less.

The instances mentioned specify soldiering and art; but one can
easily take these as representative. The sestet then declares that
Christ too was glorified through his calling and now blesses human
work done in his spirit; Christ honors such work as a "Christ-done
deed." From these thoughts it is not hard to see Hopkins's conviction of the real possibility of having a sense of calling as divine
vocation.

A sense of calling is sometimes thought of as a religious calling,
that is, the calling of a religious. Hopkins himself being in such a
calling, it is perhaps fitting to find many allusions to this kind of
calling in his poetry, especially the early and occasional pieces. An
example is "The Habit of Perfection." In this poem, the senses are
all dedicated to God and poverty is accepted as a religious virtue. I
quote the first stanza:

Elected Silence, sing to me
And beat upon my whorled ear,
Pipe me to pastures still and be
The music that I care to hear.

The religious dedicates everything to God in a specific regimen of living and finds his life's significance thereby.

Nevertheless, a sense of calling is clearly not limited only to the life of a religious. Any worthwhile occupation can be filled with a similar graciousness. There are many ways to work, many ways to feel the grace of meaningfulness.

Furthermore, the individual is also able to have a new perspective on that very world that was a context of encagement for him. Nature, from which he was alienated before, can now be seen as divine handiwork, or instress,[3] as Hopkins calls it. Man, from whom he felt isolated and estranged, can now be seen as a divine creation intended for greatness and perfection. The natural means of beauty and human association bring a person psychically closer to nature and to man, and divine grace enables him to interpret these as furnishings of God's grandeur. I would like to consider first nature and then man in Hopkins's interpretations of this grandeur. The passages cited will not be merely appreciations but rather explicit statements of divine disclosure in and through nature and man.

The *locus classicus* for this theme may, of course, be taken to be Hopkins's famous poem that stands at the beginning of his outpouring of nature poetry in 1877, "God's Grandeur." The opening lines, especially the first, trumpet the electrifying rapture of God's presence in nature:

The world is charged with the grandeur of God.
    It will flame out, like shining from shook foil;
    It gathers to a greatness, like the ooze of oil
Crushed.

Two of the poems in this series relate nature specifically to Christ and his function of making all things new and fresh and rapturous with their original perfection. All things can become hallowed by his presence in them. "The Starlight Night" says of the gorgeous things in nature:

> These are indeed the barn; withindoors house
> The shocks. This piece-bright paling shuts the spouse
>   Christ home, Christ and his mother and all his hallows.

And in "Hurrahing in Harvest," aptly titled for the mood Hopkins wishes to convey, one reads:

> I walk, I lift up, I lift up heart, eyes,
> Down all that glory in the heavens to glean our Saviour;
> . . . .
> And the azurous hung hills are his world-wielding shoulder.

Further illustrations of this profound theme of divine instress in nature, so dear to Hopkins's heart and so central to his poetry, can be found in a poem at the very beginning of his mature poetic career, another near the end, and another in the middle. In "The Wreck of the Deutschland," stanza five shows, amid the other elements of religious experience, this celebration of God's instress in nature:

> I kiss my hand
> To the stars, lovely-asunder
> Starlight, wafting him out of it; and
> Glow, glory in thunder;
> Kiss my hand to the dappled-with damson west:
> Since, tho' he is under the world's splendour and wonder,
> His mystery must be instressed, stressed;
> For I greet him the days I meet him, and bless when I understand.

In the tribute to St. Alphonsus, one of the last poems, Hopkins finds room for a parenthesis on God and nature:

> Yet God (that hews mountain and continent,
> Earth, all, out; who, with trickling increment,
> Veins violets and tall trees makes more and more).

And in "The May Magnificat," a doctrinal piece about Mary, the same connection between nature and God is made in the last stanza:

> This ecstasy all through mothering earth
> Tells Mary her mirth till Christ's birth
> To remember and exultation
> In God who was her salvation.

Even the darker, demonic aspects of nature—the so-called natural evils—can be seen as under the providence of divine benignity. There is a fine statement of this benign tolerance in one of Hopkins's early Latin poems, *"Inundatio Oxoniana."* The paradox runs, however, in various ways through much of his later poetry. Natural evil comes, but providence directs. Floods have struck Oxford, but the young poet can write (as given in prose translation): "Assuredly the pestilence has been driven away from them by a benign power, for though the west wind may renew its warm showers on our ploughlands all through the night, it vexes the recumbent acres without doing damage, and a harmless sheet of water is drawn over the fields".[4]

Man also can be seen in his magnificence when one is infused with the grace to see him so. Hopkins has much to say in his poetry about the sordidness of man, the degradation and despoiling man can instigate, the sin to which man is subject. Yet man too is a creation of goodness, and this goodness can be seen when one is released from encagement and despair to view the original instead of the spoiled copy.

If "God's Grandeur" prefaces the poetry of instress in nature, a passage from "The Handsome Heart" may be taken as the headstone for the same theme regarding man. The reference is to a child; but no matter, it is human. Christ, after all, is also revered for babehood and childhood as well as manhood. The passage is:

> Mannerly-hearted! more than handsome face—
> Beauty's bearing or muse of mounting vein,
> All, in this case, bathed in high hallowing grace.

Man, one may say, when seen at best shows the divine instress.

Elsewhere, this thought is put in terms of men's true selves that can be seen with the grace of insight. Selves are called "love's worthiest, were all known." Such true selves are the crown of creation; they can be seen, from the right perspective, to flash off the earthly bodies one contacts. They are truly "World's loveliest— Men's selves. Self flashes off frame and face" ("To What Serves Mortal Beauty?").

In the profound Scotist poem, "As kingfishers catch fire," devoted entirely to the theme of instress, one finds Hopkins's most explicit statement that man is the embodiment and vehicle of God's grace. After speaking of each mortal thing's uniqueness, the poem concludes with a sestet on man in particular:

> I say more: the just man justices;
>   Keeps grace: that keeps all his goings graces;
> Acts in God's eye what in God's eye he is—
>   Christ. For Christ plays in ten thousand places,
> Lovely in limbs, and lovely in eyes not his
>   To the Father through the features of men's faces.

Both nature and human activity are included in the justly celebrated "Pied Beauty." It is the most brilliant and yet economical statement on the theme of God's grandeur in creation. It begins with "glory be to God" for the varied magnificence of created things, and ends: "He fathers-forth whose beauty is past change:/ Praise him" (*Poems*, no. 37).

3.   *Elements of Sanctification*

Once the maintenance of one's being is ensured against the evil of negativity, once one sees meaning afresh in one's work and world, one has been readied to grow again in the spiritual life. One is drawn into deeper and more fervent awarenesses of divine grace in the process known as sanctification. Hopkins, as a Christian poet, stresses in this process the deepening awareness of God's steadfastness and a deepening personal identification with Christ.

First, what are the ways in which God's steadfastness is felt? A number of such contexts are expressed in Hopkins's poetry, though they can hardly be said to exhaust the ways for a complete phenomenology. God, after all, in the conception of him Hopkins holds may be thought of as infinitely adaptive to individual needs. The following are some of the ways God is steadfast that he alludes to in poetic context.

God is steadfast in his patience toward man's foolishness and folly. Though one may fail, "he is patient."

His steadfastness is felt as mercy toward our inability to perfect ourselves. Hopkins concludes the sonnet, "In the Valley of the Elwy," with this sentiment:

> God, lover of souls, swaying considerate scales,
> Complete thy creature dear O where it fails,
>   Being mighty a master, being a father and fond.

His steadfastness is felt as a supreme concern that every person be rescued for the fullness of being, indeed for eternal life. In "The Lantern out of Doors," Christ is referred to as having this concern. Strangers pass out of our own orbit; but in contrast:

> Christ minds: Christ's interest, what to avow or amend
>   There, eyes them, heart wants, care haunts, foot follows kind,
> Their ransom, their rescue, and first, fast, last friend.

This concern is felt not only in general but as a concern for very specific events:

> The Eurydice—it concerned thee, O Lord:
> Three hundred souls, O alas! on board.
>   ("The Loss of the Eurydice")

His steadfastness is felt in his preservation of all men's selves, from which each has felt far removed during encagement. This feeling is the theme of "The Golden Echo." The leaden lump a person may have felt himself to be during encagement has a golden original kept in God's steadfastness.

> Somewhere elsewhere there is ah well where! one,
> One. Yes I can tell such a key, I do know such a place,

> Where whatever's prized and passes of us, everything that's
>   fresh and fast flying of us,...
> . . . .
> Never fleets more, fastened with the tenderest truth
> To its own best being and its loveliness of youth: it is an ever-
>   lastingness of, O it is an all youth!

His steadfastness is felt in the sustenance of the whole natural world, and this felt experience brings us again to "God's Grandeur." This poem, by title and opening lines, appears to be about God's magnificence in nature—and it is. But as it unfolds, the poem is mainly about God's steadfastness in nature despite man's corruption of it.

> Generations have trod, have trod, have trod;
>   And all is seared with trade; bleared, smeared with toil;
> . . . .
> And for all this, nature is never spent;
>   There lives the dearest freshness deep down things;
> . . . .
> Because the Holy Ghost over the bent
>   World broods with warm breast and with ah! bright wings.

Several such themes come to bear in "The Wreck of the Deutschland." It is fitting to close these words on steadfastness by quoting from this classic, for it brings to full expression Hopkins' early religious experience and much of his later thought as well. Indeed, J. Hillis Miller refers to the poem as Hopkins's "masterwork, the poem which combines latently all the later poetry, both the poetry of nature and the poetry of the self."[5] In keeping with Hopkins's Christian realism, the poem is not a purely symbolic poem but a reflection on a concrete historical event. Nevertheless, one may appropriate the poem imaginatively, in one perspective on it, and see the wreck of the ship symbolically as a plunge into encagement. With all of the loss then at issue, God is steadfast in rescuing and in preservation. From "Part the First," stanza nine, these lines are taken:

> Be adored among men,
> God, three-numbered form;
> Wring thy rebel, dogged in den,

> Man's malice, with wrecking and storm.
> Beyond saying sweet, past telling of tongue,
> Thou are lightning and love, I found it, a winter and warm;
> Father and fondler of heart thou hast wrung;
> Hast thy dark descending and most art merciful then.

And from "Part the Second," stanzas thirty-two and thirty-three:

> I admire thee, master of the tides,
> . . . .
> Ground of being, and granite of it; past all
> Grasp God, thorned behind
> Death with a sovereignty that heeds but hides, bodes but abides;
>
> With a mercy that outrides
> The all of water, an ark
> For the listener; for the lingerer with a love glides
> Lower than death and the dark.

By way of a footnote, one should notice in these lines the phrase "ground of being" in reference to God. This phrase was made famous, of course, by Paul Tillich, with whom it is associated. It is interesting to find the term used in this great poem of 1876, before Tillich was born.

This study now turns to the second aspect of sanctification. In Christianity, the deepening awareness of divine presence may be rendered more concrete through a growing identification with Christ. This growing identification is certainly reflected in Hopkins's life and poetry. Such identification, never wholly absent in desolation but submerged under other weights, never denied doctrinally but obscured perhaps from overt attention, is now activated and heightened in the renewal of grace-filled experience. One resumes the Christian pilgrimage that looks toward an ever-progressing unity with Christ. As Hopkins writes in a fragmentary poem numbered 151 in the *Poems*:

> Hope holds to Christ the mind's own mirror out
> To take His lovely likeness more and more.

This experience of identification may have different focuses of attention and emphasis. Christ might be seen more luminously by some in his ontological status as member of the Trinity or as Mediator to man. Certainly Hopkins has passages with this focus. Or Christ may be seen more thankfully in his soteriological role as redeemer and helper, as brother and friend. Or he may be seen with moral rededication as model and example. Hopkins also writes of these meanings. But above all, perhaps the central focus for Hopkins is not that of theological statement or derived advantage, but rather a direct, simple, graceful freedom found in Christ. One is raised thereby to the freedom of graceful living. If I may be permitted to indulge in some coinages where language falters, perhaps I can say that one is "engraced" rather than encaged; one lives "grace-fully" rather than desolately.

First one can look at several passages with the theological and moral focuses and then at two superb poems in which pure identification, pure freedom in grace, is celebrated.

The penultimate stanza, stanza thirty-four, of "The Wreck of the Deutschland" is probably the most theological of Hopkins's focuses on Christ. Doctrinal considerations are first developed. But then, in a dramatic contrast, Christ's coming to man is accented in quiet tones. Though Christ partakes in God's power, "the thunder-throne," he nevertheless comes not like lightning but gently:

> Not a dooms-day dazzle in his coming nor dark as he came;
>   Kind, but royally reclaiming his own;
> A released shower, let flash to the shire, not a lightning of fire
>   hard-hurled.

This "released shower" enables one to drink deeply of refreshment, even to walk in it with relish. It is felt as the answer to the piteous plea to "send my roots rain."

Likewise in the penultimate stanza, along with the previous two, of "The Loss of the Eurydice," there is a climactic focus on Christ. In this case, the concentration is on the saving function of Christ. The passage first depicts the deep grief of the loved ones surviving the shipwreck and the inability of natural outlets (naturation) to provide the needed comfort:

> Though grief yield them no good
> Yet shed what tears sad truelove should.

But then the supervening grace of Christ is appealed to as affording a
more abiding rescue:

> But to Christ lord of thunder
> Crouch; lay knee by earth low under:
> 　　'Holiest, loveliest, bravest,
> Save my hero, O Hero savest.
>
> And the prayer thou hearst me making
> Have, at the awful overtaking,
> 　　Heard; have heard and granted
> Grace that day grace was wanted.[6]

The mediating mission of Christ is also expressed in "The Blessed
Virgin Compared to the Air We Breathe." The poet is directing his
affection here to Mary; but her role, after all, is related entirely to
Christ and his mission. She is the vehicle that

> Gave God's infinity
> Dwindled to infancy
> Welcome in womb and breast,
> Birth, milk, and all the rest
> But mothers each new grace
> That does now reach our race.

Turning to the moral role of Christ, one can also find Hopkins
identifying with Christ as a model or example for moral effort and
as a criterion for estimating the worth of human deeds. This moral
identification is illustrated in a youthful poem, "Myself unholy,
from myself unholy," in which Hopkins sees Christ as the superlative
model for measuring and dealing with human faults:

> This fault in one I found, that in another:
> And so, though each have one while I have all,
> No *better* serves me now, save *best*; no other
> Save Christ: to Christ I look, on Christ I call.
> 　　　　　　(*Poems*, no. 16)

In one of his last poems, "On the Portrait of Two Beautiful Young
People," Hopkins holds Christ up as a model and goal for young
people to follow:

> But ah, bright forelock, cluster that you are
> Of favoured make and mind and health and youth,
> Where lies your landmark, seamark, or soul's star?
> There's none but truth can stead you. Christ is truth.

In "The Soldier," Christ is viewed as somehow present in, or reflected in, the right acts and morally good acts performed by people in their earthly existence, and hence by implication as the criterion by which any such praiseworthy actions are to be measured.

> Mark Christ our King. ...
> ... There he bides in bliss
> Now, and seeing somewhere some man do all that man can do,
> For love he leans forth, needs his neck must fall on, kiss,
> And cry 'O Christ-done deed! So God-made-flesh does too:
> Were I come o'er again' cries Christ 'it should be this'.

Finally, this study considers two poems that are each integers on the present theme, celebrating identification with Christ as a simple act and not with respect to Christological functions—ontological, soteriological, or moral. In these poems there is a simple, single-minded act of commitment of one's entire person to Christ, and this unification is what is directly emblazoned in the imagery and the words of celebration.

The poem entitled "That Nature is a Heraclitean Fire and of the comfort of the Resurrection" is the poem in which the world, seen from a naturalistic standpoint, is a Heraclitean flux, with all things subject to time, death, and destruction, and human beings subject to dejection. But Christ's resurrection is then seen as the power of reversal, which interpretation can only be intended to be taken in both cosmic and personal terms. On the personal side, dejection is swept away and the merging with Christ is complete and immortal, so that what shines out alone is the "immortal diamond" that he is and that man can become through him.

In "The Windhover," Hopkins first gives a scintillating sketch of a falcon or kestral skating and swooping in the sky. The falcon then becomes a symbol for Christ in all of his earthly splendor, courage, and humanity. The identification with Christ in a very human way is thus close and complete. Addressing both falcon and Christ, the poet declares:

> Brute beauty and valour and act, oh, air, pride, plume, here
>   Buckle! AND the fire that breaks from thee then, a billion
> Times told lovelier, more dangerous, O my chevalier!

4. The Phenomenon of Joy

Joyfulness of spirit is the final flowering of the experience of grace. Therefore, the conclusion to the entire phenomenology this study has been tracing will take account of some of Hopkins's references to this experience. Joy brings a simple, victorious, exultant happiness to the process of resolution. Not that encagement is forgotten as an ever-present finite threat; not that grief is ignored as a permanent finite possibility; but these are now superseded, overcome, conquered on a new level of experience. Also, Hopkins would never think of earthly joy as complete in comparison with a final beatitude, as intimated in "Heaven-Haven"; at most it must remain penultimate and mixed with other modes of finite experience. But at least it can permeate henceforth the living out of one's life and may at times reach organlike swells and crescendos. I have quoted many stark passages from Hopkins, and certainly these have a kind of overt dominance. But Hopkins never loses his Christian vision that a joyful spirit, and not the dwelling on sin and evil, is the proper and destined fruition of human nature. Just as Christianity as a whole has sometimes been accused of having a theology of sin-consciousness at the expense of joy, so Hopkins has sometimes been interpreted as having a phenomenology of desolation at the expense of joy. Neither assessment seems just. It is well to note in conclusion, then, that Hopkins does have some overt allusions to joy and perhaps many more that are implicit.

One of the youthful unfinished poems, "Il Mystico," portends what might be called the mystery of earthly joy: earthly life seems to give grief a favored position, and yet joy wells up despite all. The poet is speaking of the prophet Ezekiel, who understood this mystery. Ezekiel is one

> Who knowing all the sins and sores
> That nest within close-barred doors,

> And that grief masters joy on earth,
> Yet found unstinting place for mirth.
>
> (*Poems*, no. 77)

The poet emulates such a capacity as a "balm to aching soul."

The joy that is this balm, this culmination of grace, may be thought of as experienced at three levels. These may be called the joy of reversal, the joy of mediation, and pure spiritual joy. The first level is mere relief in the removal of torment, or, more positively, the zest and exuberance that floods in when agony is driven out. Just as the cessation of acute pain brings, by the very reversal, a kind of pleasure, so the cessation of sorrow is the beginning of joy. The second level is the positive joy that can be mediated at any time or place through created things. God's presence is grasped within and through these things and relationships, and this presence evokes a responsive joy in the experient. John Baillie once called this experience "mediated immediacy,"[7] that is, one in which divine presence is felt as close and direct and yet as emerging through the vehicles of created things. It is especially prominent in Hopkins. The third level, pure spiritual joy, is the final, overflowing happiness in direct personal communion with God. Divine love is here the sole focus of the joyful spirit.

As an illustration of the joy of reversal, one could mention "Carrion Comfort," one of the desolation poems, in which Hopkins admits that his heart "stole joy" and could even "laugh, sheer." But a more vivid example is in "My own heart let me more have pity on," whose very structure typifies a reversal. The octave speaks of the poet's tormented mind and inability to find comfort; but the sestet enjoins a sharp change of attitude and holds up the possibility of relief through reversal. Despite his situation, the poet says to himself:

> ... let joy size
> At God knows when to God knows what; whose smile
> 's not wrung, see you; unforeseen times rather—as skies
> Betweenpie mountains—lights a lovely mile.

The possibility of joy evoked through created things has a doctrinal basis in Hopkins's view of nature as divine instress. "God's Grandeur" and "Pied Beauty" have this theme and are explicit, longer statements of it. At times Hopkins will objectify emotions like joy or bliss or ecstasy as if they were natural properties, as when, in "The May Magnificat," he speaks of "this ecstasy all through mothering earth," or when, in "Spring," he speaks of "all this joy" in nature as coming down from "earth's sweet being...in Eden garden." But these appear to be a poetic way of saying that nature is charged with divine instress and always has therefore a potential for awakening the joy that comes from knowing God, his being and acts.

Nor need anyone linger over an alleged difficulty in this conception, namely: "The special problem of Hopkins' poetry can be marked quite simply:...When a poet invokes nature as a mediating term between self and God, he faces an incipient ambiguity: is God naturalized, or is nature deified?"[8] The answer to this supposed dilemma is that neither alternative is true. God is mirrored through but does not *become* nature, and nature reflects but does not *become* God. Nature is like a mirror to the spirit's eye, and a mirror is neither the thing mirrored nor the image received. Nor does it make any of the components into another. The dilemma fails.

Two poems that brim over with this mediated joy are "Hurrahing in Harvest" and "The Woodlark." In the former, the poet, addressing his eyes and heart, asks whether anything ever "gave you a/Rapturous love's greeting of realer, of rounder replies?" And in "The Woodlark," one finds a personification of a bird's joy. The words appear to be an expression of the lark's song; but one may take them as also evincing the poet's rapture in identifying with these joyful sounds.

> 'I am so very, O so very glad
> That I do think there is not to be had
> [Anywhere any more joy to be in.
> *Cheevio*:] ...
> . . . .
> To the nest's nook I balance and buoy
> With a sweet joy of a sweet joy,
> Sweet, of a sweet, of a sweet joy
> Of a sweet—a sweet—sweet—joy.'
> *(Poems*, no. 138)

Humanly mediated joy is also part of the potentiality in creation. A particularly luminous example of this kind of joy would be the wedding ceremony, which is at once a high peak in human happiness and a sacrament of divine blessing. In his short poem, "At the Wedding March," Hopkins enjoins the couple to charity in their joy, and then, in the last stanza, turns to his own quite different wedlock, the wedlock to God, and sheds his own tearful joy:

> I to him turn with tears
> Who to wedlock, his wonder wedlock,
> Deals triumph and immortal years.
> *(Poems*, no. 52)

The human association, treated before under naturation, can, in brief, also be a vehicle through which the joy in divine presence is prompted.

Finally, all indirection and mediation are left behind and the experient has an immediate spiritual sense of the presence of God, whose nature and initiative elicit a pure spiritual joy. There is no need to think of this as mysticism, for it is a traditional part of Christian, indeed theistic, belief. Hopkins's work does not possess the kind of full-length elaborations of this experience that are so prominent concerning encagement and desolation. We would be enriched if it were so; if, in other words, the same talent which set forth a literature of desolation were enshrined in a literature of pure spiritual joy.

But the absence of such a body of mature devotional poems does not mean that this experience is absent from Hopkins's work. For one thing, Hopkins just happens to be more occupied poetically with the quest than with the culmination. Furthermore, references to God are abundant in Hopkins, forming even the very context of his work; and one may take these, however implicitly, as pointing to the final end. Most decisively, it is clear from all evidence that Hopkins never retreated from his basic Christian affirmation, and therefore one may infer that all his work is governed by the goal of reconciliation and communion with God bringing a pure spiritual joy. One may also cite the fact that there are various doctrinal and devotional pieces in Hopkins, many fragmentary, and these may be taken as pointing to joyfulness of spirit as the end.

Incidentally, and ironically, the absence of a large body of mature devotional poetry in Hopkins tends to militate against, rather than for, T. S. Eliot's stricture on Hopkins, namely, that "he is not truly a religious poet but merely a devotional poet."[9] As I am using these terms, Hopkins is not a devotional poet but a religious poet, in the sense of probing religious inquiry, interpretation, and reflection, and above all in the sense of articulating a phenomenology of the ENG experience.

One poem which, in my judgement, fairly reverberates with pure spiritual joy is "The Golden Echo." Its rhythm and words, its sound and sense, capture the buoyancy, if not the depth, of a pure spiritual joy. To read it in its entirety and aloud is to gain a measure of what this experience can be. In it there is, one might say, as much anticipation as fruition. But that is, as suggested above, the character of earthly joy. It is a culmination but yet anticipates a greater. That duality Hopkins knows and records.

Conclusion

As an epilogue to the account of grace here given, I choose some lines from a poem classified among the unfinished poems of Hopkins, although from his mature poetic period. It is not perhaps very elevated from the standpoint of poetic style; it may strike some as being a mere devotional commonplace. However, it will serve well as pointing to the practical resolution that grace completes, namely, an ongoing attempt at resilient personal living, a living in which reliance upon divine mercy is paramount, in which encagement really can be raised into conquest, and in which naturation finds its completion and fruition in a higher means. The message is that a life-pursuit like this one is still possible despite all else.

> Thee, God, I come from, to thee go,
> All day long I like fountain flow
> From thy hand out, swayed about
> Mote-like in thy mighty glow.
>
> What I know of thee I bless,
> As acknowledging thy stress
> On my being and as seeing
> Something of thy holiness.

Once I turned from thee and hid,
Bound on what thou hadst forbid;
. . . .
Spare thou me, since I see
With thy might that thou art mild.

I have life left with me still
And thy purpose to fulfil;
Yea a debt to pay thee yet:
Help me, sir, and so I will.
   ("Thee, God, I come from")

CHAPTER **V**

Illustration:
Hopkins's Life

THE PRIME illustration of one who underwent the kind of religious experience I have been describing is Gerard Manley Hopkins himself. That he should be considered here is hardly surprising since poetry comes from life. But I have avoided actually interpreting the poems biographically, not because it is unjustified, but because I have sought to isolate a general phenomenology. Now that I have done so, the account will be strengthened in concreteness by the illustration.

Some writers are not so scrupulous about a division of interests. Claude Colleer Abbott can say quite unequivocally: "The two, his work and his life, are, in the long run, inseparable."[1] There is reason in this, and I am far from saying that such an approach would be implausible if a writer's purpose were other than mine. More judicious and more subtle, however, in my judgment, is Paul Mariani's assessment: "Much of Hopkins' development is not charted in his poetry, but a careful reading of the poems reveals changes in style and in tone which have their counterpart in the man himself."[2] This statement suggests that the poetry can be seen as partially biographical provided one is extremely cautious. Great critical knowledge and the skill of a literary detective can yield a modicum of biography.

My own method in the exploration of Hopkins, however, will be far more straightforward than that of a literary detective. I shall employ the letters rather than the poems, for the former are often

97

openly in the first person and they give undoubted intimations of Hopkins's life and feelings. Again, this choice is made because my interest is neither that of a detective nor that of a biographer. I only want to show how vividly Hopkins illustrates the account I have given, and this interest is still phenomenological, albeit particularized.

It is interesting to note, as an addendum to the preceding, how tangled this issue can become, namely, the issue of the separability or inseparability of an author's life from his literary products. On the dust jacket of the volume of Hopkins's sermons and devotional writings edited by Christopher Devlin, one can find the following anonymous declaration: "But more generally interesting, and indeed fascinating, is the way in which Hopkins's writings are related to the vicissitudes of his life as a Jesuit priest; his high hopes and bitter trials; his joys and sufferings; his single-minded devotion."[3] But Devlin himself writes, in contradiction to this description: "The autobiographical element in his sermons and spiritual writings is of very little importance compared with their intrinsic interest."[4] It is not surprising that such opposite views should be taken, since they both have some merit. The only surprising thing is to find them both contained in, or in one case *on*, the same volume. But it does show the complexity of the problem. However, as I said, I shall not deal with this detective problem but shall draw direct statements from the letters for my own purpose.

Three large volumes of letters, plus some scattered others, are available to draw upon, and they are amply illustrative. There is evidence that even more material might have been available, for Abbott reports the following self-confirmed action by Bridges: "Two letters, written towards the end, he tells us that he burned, but he gives no reason. It seems probable they were letters of anguish and distress (the prose counterpart of certain of the sonnets) that he knew his friend would not wish to have printed."[5] Yet what we have is abundant and sufficient.

1.   Two Patterns in the Central Experience

There are, I believe, two principal forms that the experience of encagement, naturation, and grace takes in the religious life. One is a concentrated, short-term plunge and recovery that lasts only a few days, weeks, or months. The other is a more persistent, undulating pattern of experience that may characterize a long period of time—many years or even a lifetime. The first may be called the cataclysmic pattern and the second the chronic pattern. We might also speak of the short-term pattern and the persistent pattern, or the concentrated pattern and the undulating pattern. The first may be related more to particular occurrences, changes in circumstance, illnesses, decisions, and so on. The second may be related more to personality type, bodily and mental traits, a relatively fixed life-situation, and the like.

The two forms are not incompatible in the same person. One can be continually subject to this kind of experience and still undergo concentrated periods of especially intensive pathos. I believe that in fact Hopkins does illustrate both of these patterns in his life. It seems to me, however, that on the whole Hopkins illustrates rather more vividly the chronic pattern than the pattern of isolated occurence. He appears to have been regularly subject to depression and renewal during most of his adult life and certainly during the last twelve years or so of his life, as I shall endeavor to show.

In making this judgment, I seem to differ somewhat from Christopher Devlin, who focuses on the cataclysmic pattern, in particular on three experiences occurring, respectively, in the first half of 1883, in 1885, and in January of 1889.[6] I do not contest this view at all, since it is supportable and, as I said, the two patterns are not mutually exclusive. But I believe the testimony of the letters is too evenly distributed over Hopkins's later years to support a theory that he does not illustrate the chronic pattern more typically. Perhaps Devlin emphasizes these cataclysmic occurrences because he is working not with the letters but with notes and other writings, and extant diary notes of Hopkins do reflect his inner states during retreats that he made in the three years in question. It is true that these notes give a more intimate religious tone than do the letters. But they are to be read in conjunction with, not in opposition to, the letters. I conclude, then, that Devlin is probably right in what he maintains, as far as it goes, and accordingly this study will have a glimpse at these occurrences. But this glimpse needs to be completed by viewing the more typical chronic pattern in Hopkins's life.

2.   *The Cataclysmic Pattern in Hopkins's Life*

In the year 1883 Hopkins certainly had a spell of disheartenment. Its particular manifestations that stand out at this time are an inability to do the work he planned and a sense of stifled poetic creation. But mental anguish—the phenomenon he calls by the term "jaded"—always accompanies. He was teaching preparatory students at Stonyhurst school, and the work was not heavy, but he could not get on with anything. In March he writes to Bridges: "I am always jaded, I cannot tell why, and my vein shows no signs of ever flowing again."[7] In July he is even more outspoken. He says of himself: "I have long been Fortune's football and am blowing up the bladder of resolution big and buxom for another kick of her foot." He thinks "there is no likelihood of my ever doing anything to last." And he moans that "I am always tired, always jaded, though work is not heavy, and the impulse to do anything fails me or has in it no continuance."[8] As for his poetic impulse, his sense of stifling was apparently due in part to the attitude of his provincial, a Father Purbrick. Of this attitude Devlin says, concerning Hopkins: "It was borne in upon him that he must look on his poetic genius as an amiable weakness which a hard-working Jesuit might indulge for an hour or two occasionally."[9]

But in September of this year Hopkins attended a retreat at Beaumont where he experienced some significant renewal of spirit. It is this ten-day period that really forms the heart of this example of the cataclysmic pattern of ENG (our abbreviation henceforth for "encagement, naturation, and grace").

It is extremely interesting that Father Devlin's summary statement of this retreat experience parallels quite closely the threefold analysis that I have outlined in detail in the three preceding chapters. Since my analysis was developed fully before I read Devlin's introductions in his edition of the spiritual writings, I take his statement as independent confirmation that my general analysis is on the right track.

Hopkins underwent first a spell of desolation, then a partial illumination and recovery through fulfillment of natural aspirations, then a more complete illumination through directly felt divine grace. Devlin's summary is as follows:

> The triple pattern of the 1883 retreat should also be noted. There is a period of desolation in the "first week," followed by an abun-

dance of light and strength in the "second week"; but his final resolution from the "third and fourth weeks" is that his joy must be wholly objective, the joy of the Lord, not the fruition of his own spiritual desires.[10]

As for the first phase, or encagement, one may assume that the jaded state of previous months persisted into the retreat. Hopkins himself confirms this assumption in the second quotation below in which he speaks of being in "a desolate frame of mind." As far as the second phase, or naturation, is concerned, the following note from his diary of September 8 will give a sample of how he was attentive to those natural means of strength that were at his disposal: "I remembered Fr Whitty's teaching how a great part of life to the holiest of men consists in the well performance, the performance, one may say, of ordinary duties. And this comforted against the thought of the little I do in the way of hard penances."[11] Daily work can be regenerative. The third phase, or grace, is illustrated in a note from September 10 in which Hopkins associates his own experience with that of the two men whom Christ joined on the road to Emmaus.

> This morning in Thanksgiving after mass much bitter thought but also insight in things. And the above meditation was made in a desolate frame of mind; but towards the end I was able to rejoice in the comfort our Lord gave those two men, taking that for a sample of his comfort and them for representatives of all men comforted, and that it was meant to be of universal comfort to men and therefore to me and that this was all I really needed.[12]

So he felt a significant renewal, as is frequently the case following a retreat. As a byproduct of this renewal he felt a kind of divine assurance regarding his poetry: "he had, as he believed, a clear light from heaven that, whatever happened to his poems, they would never be a cause of hurt to himself or scandal to others." And yet this feeling was not pure, for according to Devlin: "At the same time there remained in him, against his will, a natural bitterness which he could not eradicate."[13]

The renewal itself was not long-lived. The year 1885 is well known as being perhaps Hopkins's darkest. It is sometimes alluded to as the year of blood or the year of his "dark night of the soul." His bitterest sonnets come from this year. He tells Bridges that "if ever anything was written in blood one of these was."[14] And further: "Four of these came like inspirations unbidden and against my will."[15]

Of the general state of his encagement Hopkins gives this extended account:

> And in the life I lead now, which is one of a continually jaded and harrassed mind, if in any leisure I try to do anything I make no way—nor with my work, alas! but so it must be. ... The mortification that goes to the heart is to feel it is the power that fails you.... So with me, if I could but get on, if I could but produce work, I should not mind its being buried, silenced, and going no further; but it kills me to be time's eunuch and never to beget. ... Soon I am afraid I shall be ground down to a state like this last spring's and summer's, when my spirits were so crushed that madness seemed to be making approaches.[16]

Regarding that approaching "madness" earlier in the year, Hopkins wrote to his mother, to whom he did not correspond very intimately, these euphemistic words: "I am in a sort of languishing state of mind and body, but hobble on. I should like to go to sea for six months."[17] But on the same day he gave the identical thought to Bridges more frankly: "I think that my fits of sadness, though they do not affect my judgement, resemble madness. Change is the only relief, and that I can seldom get."[18] And to his long-time college friend, Alexander W. Baillie, he had been even more outspoken a few days before:

> The melancholy I have all my life been subject to has become of late years not indeed more intense in its fits but rather more disturbed, constant, and crippling. One, the lightest but a very inconvenient form of it, is daily anxiety about work to be done, which makes me break off or never finish all that lies outside that work. It is useless to write more on this: when I am at the worst, though my judgement is never affected, my state is much like madness. I see no ground for thinking I shall ever get over it or ever succeed in doing anything that is not forced on me to do of any consequence.[19]

These passages emphasize Hopkins's sense of being thwarted, his barrenness of productivity, the nonfulfillment of his longings, his discouragement, and his mental agony. Father Devlin, in his comment on this year, gives us further insight by seeing these conditions in the light of Hopkins's sense of God's desertion.

> He himself insisted perhaps too strictly upon justice in his dealings with God; and doubts as to the acceptance of his sacrifice, accompanied by involuntary doubts about God's justice, were possibly at the root of the misery that now entangled him. Instead of being lifted to a closer union in prayer, he found himself deteriorating not only physically and mentally, but spiritually as well. ... The war was all within. ... His outraged nature (that is, his poetic genius) wreaked its revenge. ... It took ugly forms of threatened self-destruction. ... [I] t may be said to have crept into the very selfwill with which he was suppressing it.[20]

The experience of this year is not so obviously a concentrated example of ENG. Hopkins's notes from this period are scriptural comments and not personal like the retreat notes of 1883 and 1889. The letters do not contain specific accounts of illumination by naturation or grace. Devlin concludes, however, from Hopkins's revived work and interests that he did emerge from the year with a renewed spirit and that "hereafter he did live to himself more kind."[21] Indeed he does seem to have continued his work tolerably well, gotten into new studies like etymology, and composed new poetry. So one may take it that he went up rather than down in spirit, even though this episode is not so definitive a case of the cataclysmic pattern.

In addition to the work, study, and composition just mentioned—all aspects of naturation—one should remember also his persistence in spiritual discipline and in moral resolution. Right in the middle of the "madness" passages he can still say: "After all I do not despair, things might change, anything may be." This statement shows moral resolve. And again, "nobody was to blame, except myself partly for not managing myself better and contriving a change."[22] This letter shows that natural steps were open to effect at least some measure of alleviation.

As for grace, it is difficult to excerpt from the letters specific testimony from this period. In any case, more needs to be said about this phase than can be given through isolated excerpts. I shall reserve that subject for later in the chapter. One may presume from all anyone knows, however, that Hopkins felt God's steadfastness despite, or perhaps even through, the terror of the madness. Certainly he attributes to divine favor both his ability to continue at all and such light as he does possess.

When one comes in his study of Hopkins to the retreat of 1889 in Ireland, he finds another clear example of a definite, identifiable religious renewal in a brief span. The experience spreads over five days, from January 1 to 5. The first couple of days are dominated by self-loathing and the usual feelings of barrenness. Then in the next day or two one discovers hints that his attention turned to what he might do to make amends and alter things. Finally, on the fifth day once again there is the joyous light, the basking in God's illumination of his mind and will.

Here is the account from Hopkins's notes of what he felt on the first day, January 1:

> Yet it seems to me that I could lead this life well enough if I had bodily energy and cheerful spirits. However these God will not give me. The other part, the more important, remains, my inward service.
>
> I was continuing this train of thought this evening when I began to enter on that course of loathing and hopelessness which I have so often felt before, which made me fear madness and led me to give up the practice of meditation except, as now, in retreat and here it is again. ...
>
> What is my wretched life? Five wasted years almost have passed in Ireland. I am ashamed of the little I have done, of my waste of time, although my helplessness and weakness is such that I could scarcely do otherwise. And yet the Wise Man warns us against excusing ourselves in that fashion. I cannot then be excused; but what is life without aim, without spur, without help? All my undertakings miscarry: I am like a straining eunuch. I wish then for death: yet if I died now I should die imperfect, no master of myself, and that is the worst failure of all. O my God, look down on me.[23]

The next day's notes are equally morose and approach thorough despair.

> This morning I made the meditation on the Three Sins, with nothing to enter but loathing of my life and a barren submission to God's

will. The body cannot rest when it is in pain nor the mind be at peace as long as something bitter distills in it and it aches. This may be at any time and is at many: how then can it be pretended there is for those who feel this anything worth calling happiness in this life?[24]

But by the third day he begins to recover that solid common sense which tells him that what is called for on his part is not self-brooding but concerted effort. In a very startling, yet not at all sacrilegious, statement, he declares concerning his "helpless loathing": "Then I went out and I said the Te Deum and yet I thought what was needed was not praise of God but amendment of life."[25] This is naturation at work. But how should he crystallize and carry out this amendment of life in his peculiar situation—that of a teacher of Greek, a grader of exams, a foreigner in Ireland, an unswerving religious? The next day the answer becomes clear to him, and his conclusion also shows how he thinks of the natural life as fusing into the life of grace.

> And my life is determined by the Incarnation down to most of the details of the day. Now this being so that I cannot even stop it, why should I not make the cause that determines my life, both as a whole and in much detail, determine it in greater detail still and to the greater efficacy of what I in any case should do, and to my greater happiness in doing it?[26]

Finally, on the fifth day there is a flood of light and a recrudescence of spirit. Devlin's account of this restoration of spirit is particularly instructive since it also brings out the absorption of natural efforts into a flowering of grace-filled vision.

> On that same day came the deliverance, the promised "illumination" of the Second Week.... It was the light of the Epiphany broadening out... into the coming of Christ, the Way and the Light, to carry with him the sons of men. Moreover, there is a change observable in his letters after this date. His health gets worse but his spirits get better. ... They end with the cliff-face scaled and his mind and heart at one, striding forward with great strides on a high plateau of light; of light, or rather of bright shadow, in which the beloved shapes of Galilee and Judaea return once more and take their places round the radiant centre where Christ is.[27]

Hopkins lived only five months more after this retreat. He apparently reached a more steady course and a lifted spirit even before he realized the typhoid he contracted in May would be fatal. His acceptance then of this fatality was courageous and his end blissful.

There is one further point I want to reiterate concerning this last retreat experience. It is a religious experience throughout, from beginning to end, which means in this case that it is totally related to God. The experience of ENG, as I have insisted before, is not that of a would-be religious, not that of a waverer between atheism and belief in God, but a phenomenon within the life of one who is religiously committed. This is true *de dicto* of all these experiences, but this example illustrates it very well *de facto*. Thus Hopkins testifies to his allegiance to God not just at the end but from the beginning. On the first day he declares: "I do not waver in my allegiance, I never have since conversion to the Church."[28] It is God who withholds "bodily energy and cheerful spirits." It is God to whom he cries "look down on me." And he can refer in one and the same sentence to both "more loathing and only this thought, that I can do my spiritual and other duties better with God's help."[29] Such testimonies bring out the unique character of this kind of experience.

3.   *The Chronic Pattern in Hopkins's Life*

Although it is possible to point to certain specific, short-term, climactic eruptions of ENG in Hopkins's life, I believe his life illustrates better a continual susceptibility to, and varying occurrence of, this experience. This means he was regularly subject to rises and falls, expansions and contractions, in his feelings of encagement, naturation, and grace. It is a constant wave with him, sometimes more acute, sometimes abated to be sure, but always present. The lava flows in steady streams more than in volcanic explosions. The score shows more crescendo and diminuendo than triple forte.

The evidence for this assessment is twofold: direct confirmation by Hopkins and the generally spread-out testimony of the letters.

Direct confirmation by Hopkins of his long-time susceptibility is found in the letters already quoted in the previous section, though I did not quote them there for that purpose. He says, "I have long been Fortune's football." (See footnote eight.) He speaks of "the melancholy I have all my life been subject to." (See footnote nineteen.) His "loathing and helplessness" are something "I have so often felt before." (See footnote twenty-three.) His bitterness "may be at any time and is at many." (See footnote twenty-four.) These passages clearly reveal how Hopkins interprets his own life. Someone might argue that these are all encagement passages and disclose merely a melancholic temperament or disposition. It is true that they do not complete the description of the full experience. But since Hopkins did continue in his work and interests and did persist in his religious calling, one can certainly take these passages as indicative of the full range of ENG.

This interpretation is borne out amply when one considers the second kind of evidence, the spread-out testimony of the letters. These contain intimations of naturation and grace as well as encagement.

This testimony from the letters is the heart of this section of the study. I should add first, however, that I am not mainly trying to demonstrate the chronic pattern as superseding the cataclysmic pattern in Hopkins's life. That question is, after all, an interesting but entirely secondary matter. The main point throughout this chapter is that experiences in Hopkins's life, whether cataclysmic or chronic, illustrate well the full range of the religious experience outlined already from his poetry.

The life of Gerard Manley Hopkins can be viewed as falling into three distinct periods: first, his early years from 1844 to the time of his conversion in 1866 and subsequent entry into the Jesuit order in 1868; second, his Jesuit training from 1868 to 1877; and third, his priestly and teaching assignments from 1877 to his death in 1889. The first period is formative, characterized by considerable mental turmoil centering around his conversion from Anglicanism to Catholicism, but not very relevant for the kind of experience studied here. The second period finds Hopkins engrossed and apparently happy in the studies required by his chosen calling. Little extant material remains from this period with which to illustrate the ENG experience. His life appears to be a steady one in learning and in contemplation of God. With the third period, however, when Hopkins was assigned to various parts of England following his ordination, one finds almost from the beginning rumblings of those disturbances that make Hopkins's later years so illustrative of the ENG experience. The quotations of encagement cover this whole period. The only year not represented in the quotations I shall use is 1881/82, which was the year of Hopkins's tertianship during which he was once more secluded for a year of renewed study and contemplation. Thus one may take the encagement factor to be threatening to a greater or lesser degree during the entire postordination period.

Although the first period antedates the main interest of this study, it might be well to begin with two quotations from those transitional conversion years because they symbolize perhaps something of Hopkins's personality which persisted through his career. In corresponding with his father in 1866 about his conversion, something that was very painful to both of them, the son says: "It is possible even to be very sad and very happy at once and the same time."[30] This condition seems something Hopkins was destined to—a mixed life of sadness and happiness, woe and weal. It suggests also a qualitative division of ENG experiences. I have distinguished a quantitative division—cataclysmic and chronic. Now this qualitative division is that between a progressive type and an ambivalent type. The progressive type moves upward from encagement to naturation and grace, ending with sweet recovery. The ambivalent type of experience is one of encagement, naturation, and grace simultaneously and perhaps continuously throughout life. Hopkins was prone generally to the second type, it seems, although the cataclysmic examples indicate the progressive type as well. "To be very sad and very happy at once" is an elementary way of describing such deep ambivalence; but it is perhaps a presaging remark of Hopkins.

The other early quotation comes from 1868 when, upon joining the Society of Jesus, Hopkins writes to an Anglican divine, Rev. E. W. Urquhart: "Since I made up my mind to this I have enjoyed the first complete peace of mind I have ever had."[31] This sentence suggests a youth of distress, and it too may be a premonition of the kind of disposition that lends itself not only to encagement feelings but also to (let us not forget this) real states of peace of mind.

Turning to the postordination period, one finds after only a few months of his first assignment the beginning of that sense of being trapped or hemmed in with which he was to be plagued. He had been assigned to a church in Chesterfield outside London, and from here he writes to Bridges early in 1878: "Life here is as dank as ditch-water and has some of the other qualities of ditch-water."[32] Later in the same year, in his second letter to Canon Dixon, with whom he had just begun to correspond, his state of mind is also pensive: "For disappointment and humiliation embitter the heart and make an aching in the very bones."[33]

The next year finds Hopkins transferred to St. Giles Church in Oxford. Writing to Bridges again, he speaks of the lack of inspiration, or creative barrenness, of which he complains frequently henceforth. One can also detect in this letter anticipations of a desertion by God which he occasionally felt: "Feeling, love in particular, is the great moving power and spring of verse and the only person I am in love with seldom, especially now, stirs my heart sensibly and when he does I cannot always 'make capital' of it, it would be a sacrilege to do so."[34] Looking back on this Oxford work a couple of years later, he writes to another friend: "At Oxford, in my last stay there, I was not happy.... Often I was in a black mood."[35] Discouragement seems evident. And to Baillie, about that same Oxford stay, he strikes the note of alienation and isolation from others: "And in that stay I saw little of the University. But I could not but feel how alien it was, how chilling, and how deeply to be distrusted. I could have wished, and yet I could not, that there had been no one that had known me there. As a fact there were many and those friendly, some cordially so, but with others I could not feel at home."[36] From Oxford Hopkins went for a few enjoyable months to a church in Bedford Leigh near Manchester. Then in 1880/81 he is in Liverpool where he has apparently the worst experience of all so far. In the next to the last letter quoted above he refers to Liverpool as a "hellhole." And to Bridges about life there he pours out a mélange of discouragement, emptiness, weariness, and despair over human nature: "But I never could write; time and spirits were wanting; one is so fagged, so harried and gallied up and down. And the drunkards go on drinking, the filthy, as the scripture says, are filthy still: human nature is so inveterate. Would that I had seen the last of it."[37]

After Liverpool came the final year of secluded study and spiritual growth, called the "tertianship" in Jesuit training. I have already cited it as a year of relative calm and joy for Hopkins. In 1882 his work duties resumed, now in teaching, with two years at Stonyhurst school and five years at University College in Dublin. Of the desolate year 1883, already discussed in connection with the 1883 retreat, I shall add only this further lament written to Baillie in January during Hopkins's first year at Stonyhurst: "I like my pupils and do not wholly dislike the work, but I fall into or continue in a heavy weary state of body and mind in which my go is gone.... I make no way with what I read, and seem but half a man."[38]

If the 1883 retreat brought a distinct revival, it was in any case short-lived in its dispelling of the sense of encagement. For the next year he can write to Bridges out of a new onslaught of despair this stark and shocking exclamation: "AND WHAT DOES ANY-THING AT ALL MATTER?"[39] Part of the external trouble now lay, of course, in the drudgery of examinations. "I... am now drowned in the last and worst of five examinations. I have 557 papers on hand: let those who have been thro' the like say what that means."[40] But such facts are, and can only be, symptomatic, though no doubt partially causal as well, of deeply felt inner thwarting whose desolateness is so well known from this period and which we have already sampled in discussing the dark year of 1885. We pass beyond now to the last years.

If Hopkins did treat himself more kindly hereafter, he is still subject to the persistent sense of barrenness and bleakness. In 1886 he tells Canon Dixon: "It is not possible for me to do anything, unless a sonnet, and that rarely, in poetry with a fagged mind and a continual anxiety."[41]

The next year seems to be no better, for he describes in another outpouring the inertness and prostration he feels.

Tomorrow morning I shall have been three years in Ireland, three hard wearying wasting wasted years. ... In those I have done God's will (in the main) and many many examination papers. I am in a position which makes it befitting and almost a duty to write anything (bearing on classical studies).... I do try to write at it; but I see that I cannot get on, that I shall be even less able hereafter than now. ... Still I could throw myself cheerfully into my day's work? I cannot, I am in a prostration.[42]

Still the following year the drought presses on. Aridity is as dominant as ever, and this time Hopkins indicates that it is of very long standing.

> It is now years that I have had no inspiration of longer jet than makes a sonnet...; it is what, far more than direct want of time, I find most against poetry and production in the life I lead. Unhappily I cannot produce anything at all.... All impulse fails me: I can give myself no sufficient reason for going on. Nothing comes: I am a eunuch—but it is for the kingdom of heaven's sake.[43]

The tone of isolation is again sounded as well: "It appears I want not scenery but friends."[44]

The last months of Hopkins's life in 1889 I have already touched on.

This brief chronological selection from the letters illustrates well, I think, most of the themes of encagement outlined in chapter two, at least in general form. The only theme of which I can find no direct expression in the letters is that of world-sorrow. There is perhaps a hint of this theme in the quotation below. This quotation, which is really not about suicide but about the dreadfulness of our times, indicates not that Hopkins ever considered suicide but rather a certain sorrow over the state of the world. "Three of my intimate friends at Oxford have thus drowned themselves, a good many more of my acquaintances and contemporaries have died by their own hands in other ways: it must be, and the fact brings it home to me, a dreadful feature of our days."[45] And it is very interesting indeed that David Downes uses the term "world-sorrow" in characterizing Hopkins's melancholic nature. His view is that this melancholy was lifelong but that it reached a crescendo in the last years.

> Anyone who reads through the writings of Gerard Manley Hopkins will certainly be struck by what might be described as an essential sorrow that was so much a part of Hopkins's life and which is so often the tone and theme of his poetry. Many readers know his sonnets of 1885-89 in which the sorrow becomes the sorrow of a Lear or Hamlet, a universal sorrow that is both sublime and purgative. Despite the suggestions of some critics, it is clear that from the

beginning Hopkins was essentially an idealist who could not but be downcast over the world. And this "world-sorrow" increased during his life until the last four years when it became a real desolation.[46]

Thus the first of the phases of ENG has, I think, been amply illustrated from Hopkins's life. What about the second?

It is evident from the letters and other sources of knowledge that Hopkins undertook a variety of natural employments which had the effect of countering the debilitating features of encagement. It is not possible to pick out from the letters examples from every year to illustrate each of the means discussed in chapter three. But it is possible to illustrate all of the means at some time or other from the corpus and to extrapolate as a reasonable hypothesis that they were pretty much available to him throughout his life and fairly constant aids to him in his struggles. I turn then from a more chronological sequence of documentation in the case of encagement to a more thematic mode in the case of naturation.

Hopkins's love of beauty is the natural means that is least in need of documentation because it is virtually synonymous with his name as a poet. Known universally are his keen sensitivity to and appreciation of the sensuous qualities of nature and his further absorption into more formal, intellectual, and spiritual aspects of beauty as well. What is not so much emphasized is that his immersion in the sensuous elements of nature is something that characterized him from his early years to the end of his life. The other dimensions of beauty were apparently, as might be expected, more matters of growing and maturing interest. For instance, his journals from his college and early Jesuit years are devoted almost entirely to sensuous descriptions of natural things.[47] Yet his Oxford dialogue on the origin of beauty and his comments on theological and philosophical topics during these years clearly testify that his aesthetic interests were hardly limited to the sensuous.[48]

As far as direct testimony of the letters is concerned, they are so loaded with discussions of poetry and music and nature that one cannot doubt for a moment that beauty was a profound and lifelong preoccupation of Hopkins. I shall quote only one excerpt in which he reflects discriminatingly on the subject of beauty.

I think then no one can admire beauty of the body more than I do.... But this kind of beauty is dangerous. Then comes the beauty of the mind, such as genius, and this is greater than beauty of the body and not to call dangerous. And more beautiful than beauty of the mind is beauty of character, the "handsome heart."... Though even bodily beauty... is from the soul, in the sense, as we Aristotelian Catholics say, that the soul is the form of the body, yet the soul may have no other beauty, so to speak, than that which it expresses in the symmetry of the body.[49]

This passage, and the poem "To what serves Mortal Beauty?" as well, illustrates that Hopkins's interest in beauty was not only appreciative and artistic but also philosophical and theological.

Beauty is not thought of as a healing balm by Hopkins or any other artist—not overtly at least. And yet it has that function, and there is a nice sentence from Dixon which emphasizes both the beauty and the healing he finds in Hopkins's poetry. He says that "in the power of forcibly *and* delicately giving the essence of things in nature, *and* of carrying one out of one's self with healing, these poems are unmatched."[50]   One may be sure that his healing of beauty was a forcible and delicate potion in Hopkins's own life.

Hopkins's poetic output and musical efforts testify that artistic expression was also a prime natural antidote in such mental well-being as he was able to have. Some critics have written as if this urge to create was his problem rather than an uplifting release from it. But there would surely be "false cause" reasoning in such a contention. Hopkins complained often and bitterly about his *inability* to produce, implying that the *ability* to produce was what his being craved. One cannot then say that the ability to produce was the problem; no, it was part of the solution. It is true that if he had no genius, he would not be confronted with this particular element in his despair. But this is not to say that such genius, or its actual expression, is itself the drawback. Blockage of genius is a problem; but expression of genius is a solution. And Hopkins had some measure of solution, some wholesome relief, in this regard, despite his complaints. Abbott states the matter well in one of his introductions. Speaking of the last poems in particular, he writes:

These poems are salt with the taste of his blood and bitter with the sweat of his anguish, the work of a man tried to the utmost limit of his strength and clinging to the last ledge where reason may find a refuge. Their authority and truthfulness cannot be questioned. Here,

indeed, is a chart of despair, agony, and frustration, made by one
who still believes in the justice of God. That the chart was mapped
at all shows how urgent was the need for self-expression to alleviate,
even though it could not resolve, his conflict.

Though beaten to his knees, though he has wrestled with God
and not prevailed, some strength is left to him still.[51]

Professor Mackenzie makes a similar point while using a specific
illustration: "If he turned from Tom Heart-at-ease to his own pitiful
storm-drenched, cliff-clinging soul, he could also turn back again to
complete the verbal subtleties of that sonnet on the unemployed."[52]
That Hopkins himself placed a very high personal and educative
value upon artistic expression is clear from the following quotation:
"It was by providence designed for the education of the human race
that great artists should leave works not only of great excellence
but also in very considerable bulk."[53] Consequently, in the same
letter he urges Patmore on to creation (and is he also perhaps speaking
to himself?): "You will never be younger; if not done soon it will
never be done, to the end of eternity. Looking back afterwards you
may indeed excuse yourself and see reasons why the work should
not have been done—but it will not have been done, what might
have been will not exist. This is an obvious and a homely thought,
but it is a good one to dwell on."[54]

It is important to note also that creative expression does not here
mean art exclusively. There are many ways of creative self-expression
which are open to mankind. Hopkins, for instance, had a variety of
academic interests, besides his artistic ones, which he kept alive. It
is in connection with one of these that he gives one of the most
direct statements of the value he attaches to such activity. Right in
the midst of his Dublin depression and heavy work, he nevertheless
takes time to work on an etymological paper for a learned society.
He declares, almost jubilantly: "I have asked and obtained leave to
read my paper at the next meeting and have written most of it.
Writing it has naturally cleared my mind and indeed opened out a
sort of new world."[55] There can be no doubt that such creative
efforts of various kinds were very helpful in keeping Hopkins on a
steady keel despite his anguish.

Of Hopkins's moral steadfastness and fortitude, Gardner has this
apt comment: "Even in the poems of desolation the note of heroic

resistance, or Stoic acceptance, or willing surrender to the higher necessity, is more marked than the tone of weak self-pity."[56] Although this passage emphasizes the Stoical side of morality, which was perhaps the fundamental need in Hopkins's circumstances, one should not think of Hopkins's moral concern as consisting entirely of the negative duty of acceptance. He was positively devoted to charity and the other virtues, keenly interested in social and national issues, deeply moved by the needy and the sick. His wholehearted allegiance to the moral life is brought out in the following aphorism written to Patmore: "It seems to me we should in everything side with virtue, even if we do not feel its charm, because good is good."[57]

That this moral resolve has a basis in natural reason, and is therefore a real possibility in naturation, is amply evident in the correspondence with Robert Bridges. Hopkins could not write to Bridges as a Catholic, or even as an obvious Christian, or even as a clear theist. He had to appeal to natural reason and not to faith or common dogmas. At one stage, for instance, Hopkins proposes a moral course for Bridges which is supposed to be a "counsel open to no objection" on rational grounds. What is this moral course? "It is to give alms." For the giving of alms "changes the whole man, if anything can; not the mind only but the will and everything."[58] Moral resolve can thus be a vital catalyst not only in the environment in which action occurs but in the agent who may be in dire need of renovation. Hopkins himself certainly exemplifies moral dedication.

The letters give us a picture of Hopkins busily and dutifully engaged in his assigned tasks despite his complaints that he could not do them as thoroughly as he wished. Harrassed as he was, he did perform his assignments, he did prepare those sermons, he did pursue study and training, he did grade those exams. Except for brief vacations, he was regularly at work doing the best he could in his labors. There are no periods of total lethargy, confinement, or convalescence with which to cope. Daily work was another of the stabilizing pivots in his conflict.

Nor should one think of his daily work solely as routine drudgery. When he was assigned to be a professor of Greek in Dublin, he went beyond the call of pedagogical duty. He investigated Greek meter, diction, and etymology. He branched out into Egyptian etymology. There is an interchange on these matters with his friend Baillie which spreads over many letters and postcards.[59] This and other instances of the same sort exemplify how daily work, done with dedication and some imagination and not simply disgust, has a recuperative potential for the agent.

Isolation from others is one of the elements of encagement Hopkins suffered. And yet there were human associations too that were of great restorative value to him. Though generally distant from his family because of his conversion, he retained his familial affection and had a special rapport with one of his sisters. Though not particularly close, apparently, to the members of his order, he speaks of some of his superiors and brothers with warmth. Though often alienated from the cities where he dwelt, he had some congenial individual friends. For example, though feeling unhappy during his church assignment at Oxford, he nevertheless writes to a friend, Francis de Paravicini, that "there were many consolations and none pleasanter than what came from you and your house."[60] Again, though he felt alienated in Liverpool and Dublin, Hopkins speaks with fondness about the people of Bedford Leigh near Manchester, where he spent a few months in 1879. Comparing this place with Oxford, he says: "With the Lancastrians it is the reverse; I felt as if [I] had been born to deal with them."[61] Again, though he could not share in or sympathize with the mode of life which most people of his time indulged in, and in fact thought modern civilization to be in pretty bad shape, he nevertheless had compassionate feelings for all victims and sufferers. For instance, he could, in commenting on one of his poems, write:

> But presently I remember that this is all very well for those who are in, however low in, the commonwealth and share in any way the common weal; but that the curse of our times is that many do not share it, that they are outcasts from it and have neither security nor splendor; that they share care with the high and obscurity with the low, but wealth or comfort with neither.[62]

Convivial human associations seem for Hopkins, as they probably are generally, harder to come by than the more tangibly available naturations like appreciation of beauty and performance of daily work. Yet he craved them and valued them enormously when they emerged. The letters themselves were instruments of affection for him, keeping alive the contacts of comradeship. They show affection as well as poetic criticism, scholarship, biography, and much else. As a symbol of this affection I shall include a typical closing greeting. It is from one of the last letters to Bridges:

> With kind love to Mrs. Bridges and Mrs. Molesworth, I am your affectionate friend
>
>   Gerard[63]

Finally, the precious esteem in which Hopkins prized human friends and affection is shown in the following excerpt from a letter sent to Baillie less than a year before Hopkins died: "I think, and may have said before, that you did not always fully appreciate their merit in this regard; but now at your present age, much the same as mine, you are aware that affection, no matter from whom it comes, is a precious thing and not to be found at random."[64]

The habit of spiritual discipline was for Hopkins, as a religious, partly equivalent with daily work. His entire adult life was very much informed by spiritual discipline. He apparently did the prescribed exercises willingly and regularly even if his spirits waned and his human roots ran dry. He certainly regarded them as important for his well-being as well as for their religious significance. There is little in the letters about them since the letters are to outside friends and not about intra-Jesuit matters. His retreat notes give a little more characterization, as already indicated. Retreats were of special value to him. But persistence in prayer was perhaps the most vital spiritual discipline to stand out.

Nor need one think of spiritual discipline as doing prescribed exercises only, any more than morality is limited to formal duty. Take almsgiving, for instance, already mentioned: "Everybody knows...how it feels to be short of money, but everybody may not know...how it feels to be short of money for charity's sake. ... It is a noble thing and not a miserable something or other to give alms and help the needy and stint ourselves for the sake of the unhappy and deserving."[65] Certain moral and secular activities can, then, be done for spiritual discipline as well as for their natural value. And "how it feels" to do this can be efficacious in overcoming desolation and was so for Hopkins.

I concluded the account of naturation in chapter three with intellect and wit considered as additional means. These were also resources for Hopkins personally. Intellectual activity was a sustaining interest throughout his entire career. He was an honors student and a university graduate; he had long seminary training in theology and philosophy; he taught in the liberal arts; he wrote and wanted to write more in classical studies and other subjects; he familiarized himself with poetic tradition; his letters show him conversant with modern culture, politics, arts, and letters. Intellect is one of the more obvious of his capacities.

Humor, on the other hand, is perhaps Hopkins's least-known trait. Yet he seems to have retained a lively sense of wit throughout his difficulties. Gardner reminds us that "we must not suppose that he was *always* melancholy. He could be playful and witty."[66] In fact: "He never lost his sense of humor."[67] A Jesuit associate of Hopkins, Father C. Bowen, reflecting on Hopkins some thirty years after the poet's death, says of him: "He was a delightful companion, full of high spirits and innocent fun."[68]

Apparently Hopkins could be so jocular at times that he ran into a little opposition for it. He writes to Bridges about the matter: "I am ill today, but no matter for that as my spirits are good. ... I have it now down in my tablets that a man may joke and joke and be offensive; I have had several warnings lately.... And here I stop, for fear of it ripening into some kind of joke."[69]

He gives us some puns in a letter to Baillie:

> I shall therefore end with some jeux d'esprit.... What woman had more husbands than even the one that had seven husbands?—The woman that was Lot's wife. What difference has the Land League made to an Irish landlord?—Only this, that before he had an income in his rents, while now he has rents in his income. If you put your head aside at the proper angle these are good jokes.[70]

It is interesting that one of the first recollections of Canon Dixon, Hopkins's schoolmaster at Highgate, upon the renewal of their acquaintance in 1878, was of humorous incident. Dixon writes: "I remember that we once laughed together over some not very laudatory criticism which you passed at table upon 'Father Prout.'"[71]

There is some cause-and-effect ambiguity about humor. Is humor an *effect* of good recovery already gained and not possible without it, or can humor be an aid in *causing* some recovery? Probably there is some truth in both. If there is any truth at all in the latter, then Hopkins had, in wit, an ample natural boon at his disposal.

One may conclude that all of the means of naturation discussed before were utilized by Hopkins to combat his desolation. But were they sufficient?

No. This must be the answer if the matter is viewed from direct testimonial. Hopkins is unswervingly loyal to his conviction that natural means are efficacious only because they are made possible by, are preparatory for, and are completed in divine grace and favor. There are not many descriptions of this intimate experience in the letters since, as mentioned before, they are mainly to outsiders on secular topics. The spiritual diaries give us some accounts, and the sermons tell us his interpretations and applications of grace theologically. It seems best not to try to illustrate this experience as I have the previous stages, but to try to intimate its power in his life by citing the evidence upon which this contention can be based. In a word, my mode of documentation here will be not chronological or thematic but will instead be systematic.

There are five types of evidence, at least, on which the judgment of the power of grace in Hopkins's life can be based. These are: his allegiance to the Church, his affirmation of divine guidance, his identification with Christ, his view of nature, and testimonials about his life.

As quoted before, Hopkins never wavered in his allegiance to the Church. He shared regularly and conscientiously in the means of grace mediated through the Church. All of his natural efforts of will were integrated into this context as the prime vehicle for regeneration, not only theologically viewed but psychologically too. Thus his whole life as a religious testifies to the primacy of grace in the ENG experience which he underwent.

But one also finds Hopkins witnessing to direct and personal divine guidance in life. Grace is received in personal ways and not only through the more formal or prescribed means. In a letter to Dixon he gives inspired utterance to this conviction:

> When a man has given himself to God's service, when he has denied himself and followed Christ, he has fitted himself to receive and does receive from God a special guidance, a more particular providence. This guidance is conveyed partly by the action of other men,

as his appointed superiors, and partly by direct lights and inspirations. If I wait for such guidance, through whatever channel conveyed, about anything, about my poetry for instance, I do more wisely in every way than if I try to serve my own seeming interests in the matter. ... To live by faith is harder, is very hard; nevertheless by God's help I shall always do so.[72]

This is an eloquently simple and personal affirmation. In another letter to Dixon also written during his seclusion of the year of tertianship at Roehampton, he expresses a deep and serene desire for a singleminded devotion to God. He says that "my mind is here more at peace than it has ever been and I would gladly live all my life, if it were so to be, in as great or a greater seclusion from the world and be busied only with God."[73] Such statements as these testify directly to the personal reception of divine grace.

Moreover, Hopkins submitted himself in an earthly way as well as in theological belief to the life of Christ, and this submission was a source of great strength as a mode of grace. He saw his own situation—one of seeming failure and yet ideally one of success through failure—as epitomized in the life of Christ through whom he could therefore derive comfort and strength by identification of spirit. This identification did not bring "consolation" in the technical sense of an antithesis to "desolation," for it did not simply eliminate all desolation. Yet it brought strength for living this finite life and an assurance of consolation. I suggest that this way indicates how one is to read the following passage of identification which Hopkins wrote to Dixon: "Above all Christ our Lord:... he was doomed to succeed by failure; his plans were baffled, his hopes dashed, and his work was done by being broken off undone. However much he understood all this he found it an intolerable grief to submit to it. He left the example: it is very strengthening, but except in that sense it is not consoling."[74] This passage illustrates very well, I believe, the unique and paradoxical character of Hopkins's religious experience; and it therefore helps to demarcate the distinctiveness of the ENG pattern of experience. Hopkins experiences grace—a basic and common Christian experience—but he feels it with distinctive nuances deriving from the lingering, never-banished shadows of encagement.

A further consideration that is relevant to an understanding of Hopkins's experience is his view of nature itself, that is of everything natural. His view is that nature cannot stand by itself but is in essence a mirror of divine splendor and majesty. Gardner says he displays "a Wordsworthian feeling for nature and man" which is in turn "heightened by his view of the world as 'word, expression, news of God.'"[75] This view is so associated with Hopkins that his line "The world is charged with the grandeur of God" is now virtually classic for it.

Applying this to naturation or natural methods of liberation from encagement, one may say that these means, when functioning at their best, will lead to or reveal God's grandeur behind all existence. This statement does not mean that nature is nothing and grace is everything, for that would suggest that God initiates all actions and man initiates none by his own volition. We do initiate acts by our will, and this act of will makes naturation real and not perfunctory. But everything natural opens out ultimately to the divine source. Nature is completed by grace. Hopkins sees all of his own efforts as made possible by, and as fulfilled in, the One he single-heartedly serves.

Finally, as evidence for the grace-filled experience of Hopkins, one can turn to testimonies about his character as a person and as a religious aspirant. Mariani speaks for many in this regard when he says: "Whatever desolation and isolation Hopkins experienced at the end of his short life (he died at forty-four), one thing is clear: he was growing steadily closer to the condition of sainthood."[76] Another writer is less restrained and goes so far as to say of Hopkins that "he was within a stone's throw of being a saint—by any standard, human or divine."[77]

But let us turn to two contemporaries of Hopkins, one of whom knew him from school days, and the other of whom met him only later in life. These friends also differ—and this difference makes their testimony the more striking—in their opinion of Hopkins's Jesuit affiliation. It is striking because, though they differ about this affiliation, they nevertheless agree in their estimate of Hopkins's saintly character. First, an Anglican critic of Jesuit discipline writes to Hopkins's brother a year after the poet's death:

> Humanly speaking he made a grievous mistake in joining the Jesuits for on further acquaintance his whole soul must have revolted against a system which has killed many and many a noble soul; but what matters the means compared with the undoubted result. Any

wood will do for the cross, when God's perfection is thereby reached. To get on with the Jesuits you must become on many grave points a machine, without will, without conscience, and that to his nature was an impossibility. To his lasting honor be it said he was too good for them, as he was for Dyne in his boyhood, and no earthly success could ever compare with the crown he has won and now wears.[78]

But let the final appraisal be the beautiful tribute of a Catholic friend and poet, Coventry Patmore. Just after Hopkins's death, he writes to Bridges:

Gerard Manley Hopkins was the only orthodox, and as far as I could see, saintly man in whom religion had absolutely no narrowing effect upon his general opinions and sympathies. A Catholic of the most scrupulous strictness, he could nevertheless see the Holy Spirit in all goodness, truth, and beauty; and there was something in all his words and manners which were at once a rebuke and an attraction to all who could only aspire to be like him.[79]

These evidences indeed testify to the reality of grace in Hopkins's experience, and all of the citations in this chapter collectively confirm him as a prime illustration of the ENG experience. The poet is father to the poems.

CHAPTER **VI**

Problems of
Interpretation

HAVING DESCRIBED and illustrated the ENG experience in some
detail, I shall turn in this chapter to the critical task of examining
certain questions of interpretation regarding this central experience
in Hopkins's poetry. Again my primary concern will be with how the
general type of experience might be interpreted and not with views
of Hopkins himself as a person. These two will be harder to separate
in a discussion of this kind, since many of the theories I shall criti-
cize as general interpretations of the experience are taken from
material intended in the first place as comment on Hopkins himself.
Therefore, one cannot be too rigid about the distinction. Furthermore, a judgment about Hopkins himself that is correct (or incorrect) may very well not be correct (or incorrect) as a generalized
interpretation. Nevertheless, my main goal is to evaluate certain
possible interpretations of the general experience.

There are two principal questions of interpretation that dominate
the scene of Hopkins studies dealing with this experience. One is
concerned with the cause of the experience. What brings about the
ENG experience; for example, what caused it in Hopkins' life?
The other question focuses on essential classification. What is the
essence of the experience; that is, of what *kind* or *type* is it? Where
shall we place it among the many sorts of experiences, religious or
otherwise, which humanity has? In older terminology, these con-

cerns may be called the problem of efficient cause and the problem of formal cause. To carry the language further, one could say that the material cause has been given in the foregoing phenomenology of elements composing the experience. This statement would leave remaining the question of final cause, that is, the purpose or end served by the ENG experience. I believe this question to be finally a theological question that carries one beyond the present phenomenological study. Some remarks will be offered on it, however, by way of conclusion; but first this study will turn to the two problems of cause (in the modern sense) and classification.

1.   *The Problem of Cause*

The question of what causes, or can cause, the ENG experience becomes a philosophical question when one asks what sorts of causes are to be admissible as possibilities. The answer will depend much on one's metaphysical perspective.

Three groups of causes have been claimed as the origin of Hopkins's own experience and by implication of the ENG experience in general. These may be called physical causes, mental causes, and spiritual causes. No doubt the last two could be considered variations of mental events. Materialistic psychologists would subsume all three under physical events. But I shall follow the ordinary language distinction between physical and mental events and shall consider spiritual events to be a special case of the latter which involves a religious construction. Mental causes, in short, will be construed as natural events, and spiritual causes will be construed as mental events seen as related specifically to extranatural or divine power. It is thus obvious from this scheme that the ultimate analysis of causes will depend partly on how one interprets the reality of matter, mind, and spirit.

First, physical causes: A number of physical ailments and circumstances have been suggested as the causes that brought about Hopkins's later experience. These explanations have concentrated on his desolation and despondency, and thereby reveal one of the limitations of this kind of explanation; for while it is possible to cite harsh physical conditions as bringing about difficulties, it is more dubious to identify physical factors in Hopkins's life that would generate the recoveries he felt through naturation and grace. Among the physical causes often mentioned are a delicate sort of constitution, a physically based condition of neuresthenia, the laborious requirements of examination grading, specific physical surroundings such as slums, and general weariness of body. Concerning the ENG experience in general, which anyone might undergo, one could easily add other physical causes: for example, diseases, chronic painfulness, overwork, underwork, immobility of various kinds, disagreeable surroundings, accidental deaths and injuries, and so on. But these, too, like the others, seem to focus on how a person might be plunged into despair rather than on how one is elevated into restoration. Of course someone could argue that if physical causes can generate the desolation, then the reversal of those causes could initiate the removal of desolation. True enough, but this assertion may simply be a good reason for questioning the adequacy of physical explanations at either end of the ENG experience. Harsh physical conditions do not always generate despondency among the spiritually committed; indeed examples to the contrary abound. Nor do pleasant physical circumstances always offset a drift toward despair. It seems, therefore, that while one must recognize physical causes as important in personal experience, one must not grant to them the position of universal explanation. This caution is true even at the encagement level and would seem to be still more the case at the recovery level.

Second, mental causes: Some other interpreters attribute the experience to some kind of mental disequilibrium. One example of this would be the view that Hopkins was to some degree mentally isolated from his age and this produced in him severe anxiety. John Wain upholds this view as quoted in the following passage:

> So why speak of desperation? The answer is that the desperation was in the loneliness. Only someone who was completely alone could have produced an art that takes so little and gives so much. For Hopkins, the struggle of creation must have been agonizing; and the incomprehension which met his work must often have numbed his entire being. ... His isolation removed him from the hubbub of the market-place and enabled him to listen in silence to the messages which came from the real spirit of his age. Yet the deep-seated inability to trade in that market-place also involved him in disappointment, humiliation, and weariness.[1]

Now I have already spoken of personal isolation from others as an element in encagement, and it could well be partly cause and partly effect. But isolation from one's age is another matter. It seems that some people could feel this very acutely and it could have a grave effect upon them. Whether this is so of Hopkins is more questionable, since he found his true spiritual home in the Church, which he thought of in opposition to the secular age that surrounded him. Isolation from that age would then be something to be expected. Actually the recent studies of Hopkins as a Victorian[2] would tend to militate against this extreme isolationist view on straight empirical grounds. Moreover, there is some evidence that Hopkins was not bothered much about whether or not he was in tune with the surrounding world. In one letter to Dixon he could write: "Besides all which, my mind is here more at peace than it has ever been and I would gladly live all my life, if it were so to be, in as great or a greater seclusion from the world and be busied only with God."[3] Dixon's reply confirms this impression about Hopkins: "I can understand that your present position, seclusion and exercises would give to your writings a rare charm."[4] Nevertheless, one must not ignore this isolation as a factor in Hopkins's later stay in Ireland, and in any case it may be an enervating factor for other religious believers in other times and places.

Another sort of psychological explanation was suggested by Herbert Read in the thirties. He subsumes the case of Hopkins under a more general psychological problem faced by creative minds, namely, the mental conflict between emerging creative thought and the pool of inherited ideas in society.

> We are born with sensibility and come into a world of ready-formulated ideas. ... The space between self and dogma is... bridged by doubt. My contention is that a creative gift or poetic sensibility is only consistent with such a state of spiritual tension and acuity. True originality is due to a conflict between sensibility and belief.... The evidence is clear to read in all genuine mystics and poets; and nowhere more clearly than in the poetry and mysticism of Gerard Hopkins.[5]

The mystical part I shall discuss later. The doubt about dogma was certainly a cause of turmoil in Hopkins's conversion period. But then this doubt was settled in his mind, and there seems no reason to think it loomed again. Some tendency to think of desolation as necessarily involving dogmatic doubt does exist. But such doubt seems more characteristic of conversion experience than of ENG experience. Yet mental conflicts of one sort or another may heighten the desolation felt by some people.

Another explanation is that Hopkins underwent some kind of neurosis or mental disorder in late years. Gardner, for instance, says that "religious apologists have underestimated the agonies of failure and frustration which creative genius, without any religious complications, can undergo; they seem to have ignored the neuroses which may be caused when powerful instincts and impulses are repressed or imperfectly satisfied."[6] An even stronger statement of this explanation is given in the following words: "Aggravated by bodily weakness, his constitutional melancholia begins to show itself in an acute form which bordered, as he said, on madness, though his judgment was never impaired."[7] In his second volume, Gardner speculates further on this mental disorder and suggests that a more specific cause for it might be found in a certain lack of self-understanding in Hopkins: "it seems to us that his lack of balance consisted in his inability to recognize his own congenital limitations."[8]

Some weight must certainly be given to such a condition in Hopkins, for he does complain at times about a feeling approaching madness. Our continuing question, however, concerns the adequacy of any one alleged cause. It begins to look as if many causal factors can, singly or in combination, initiate the ENG experience.

Also one should not focus solely on the initial phase of the experience, even though it is often the most dramatic and even though it can to some extent be distinguished for separate analysis. One does have, however, in mental causes, what would seem to be an indispensable factor for the later phases of the experience, especially the processes of naturation. That is, if naturation really consists of self-initiated phases of partial recovery, it is hard to see how this could occur unless there is genuinely efficacious power of will. Here the mind's affirmations and the will's efforts must be instrumental in the experience. Further, it seems reasonable, though not a necessary implication, that if various physical and mental causes can produce the initial desolation, then their removal and positive replacement could be contributory to recovery. Thus a pluralism of causation again seems indicated, at least for the first two phases, encagement and naturation.

As far as grace is concerned, a theological or metaphysical position is prerequisite. One could not interpret the grace experience in its literal signification without believing that there is divine causation involved. If one does not accept this, then one would seek the causal explanation of this phase of the experience in heightened versions of the preceding types of physical and mental causes, stressing either self-induced recovery or unusually affable outer conditions.

Third, spiritual causes: Although it is a somewhat loose distinction, spiritual causes can be thought of as those mental events that are interpreted as already overladen with allusion to extranatural reality in contrast to natural phenomena alone. An example would be the concept of sin in contrast to that of mistakes.

A rather simple explanation of this sort is given Hopkins's experience by Robert Andreach. He says that "what is fundamental in Hopkins's work [is] the sense of pride, which is a hindrance to spiritual growth."[9] The causal factor here then is prideful self-will, the inflation of the ego, which prevents openness and humbleness toward God. This egoism is what lies behind the struggle which the experient undergoes in his desolate experience. Andreach summarizes: "The cause of that struggle is the persistence of selfhood, the refusal to abandon totally the will to God's will, the failure to achieve complete self-abnegation and humiliation."[10]

Aside from the fact that the focus is again on the first phase of the experience, this condition of man is certainly something that must be taken seriously as an explanation if one accepts spiritual causes as operative. It is, after all, the state whose cure is what religion, from one point of view, is all about. As a causal account of the ENG experience in particular, however, it may apply more to hosts of other people than to Hopkins himself. There is little reason to think he was obstinate in will and greatly lacking in humility and charity. Hopkins himself might agree to such a self-condemnation, but here is a case where one's own testimony might not be the most reliable since it is notorious that the best of men often think of themselves as the worst of sinners. Furthermore, there seems no obvious reason why a person could not be far along in spiritual humility, obedience, charity, and so on, and still be victimized by various physical and mental onslaughts. Witness Job. So again the pluralism of causes stands out.

A very insightful interpretation of Hopkins is suggested by Howard Fulweiler in a recent work comparing Arnold and Hopkins. Recognizing a multiplicity of causes, the author takes as paramount Hopkins's struggle with a dynamic and changing Christian outlook. According to this view, Hopkins was not as orthodox in thought as is commonly supposed but was seeking to find new Christian formulations and the language to express them. "Admitting the many possible causes of Hopkins' unhappiness," Fulweiler says, "I should like to continue viewing Hopkins as an innovative thinker wrestling with an evolving Christian theology and an evolving theory of the imagination."[11] Hopkins would thus be like many a modern Catholic— or members of other faiths for that matter—at home in their Church but seeking to reject certain older stances and to reformulate certain theological dogmas in an ongoing process of evolving thought-forms. In Hopkins's case this changing Christian outlook sets up a powerful tension within his soul that can even be described as a war within. In a final summation the author writes:

> Not only was the struggle between God and Hopkins; it was also between two separated personalities of Hopkins: Hopkins as Christ, immanent and creative in man and nature; Hopkins as Lucifer, animated by "will unwavering," but alienated from God by pride in himself and in his art. What made the tension even more unbearable was that sometimes Hopkins identified the creative personality as *Satanic* and the strong-willed personality as *Christ-like*. ... In the continuing war between these apparently irreconcilable versions of the self lie the causes of Hopkins' personal agony. His "war within" is also a parable of nineteenth-century intellectual history in its theological struggle against deism and its literary struggle to re-establish the language of poetry in the modern world.[12]

That Hopkins underwent, like all persons, a personal spiritual pilgrimage, that he did so more intently and more intensely than most people, that his seeking of God directed his life, there can be no doubt. But that he had any quandary about orthodox Catholic belief is very questionable. He seems not to have dealt with orthodox belief except to affirm it, to apply it, and occasionally to speculate in those areas where dogma was not fixed and where speculation was admitted and invited. Nevertheless, one has in this notion of ongoing spiritual pilgrimage a general framework (however it stands with Hopkins himself) for understanding how it would be very likely to have the ups and downs, the uncertainties and triumphs, the dryness and rainfall characteristic of the experience studied here. The soul is restless until fruition appears, and restlessness is prone to downfall and recovery.

In overall conclusion, it seems best to hold that there are various physical, mental, and spiritual causes involved in the ENG experience. Some of these physical and mental causes are outside one's will and generate both enervating and restorative effects upon us. Self-will must be included among mental causes if naturation is genuinely operative. Spiritual causes can be operative in all phases of the experience and are especially important as initiating the only human causation at the third phase, namely, an openness to or preparedness for divine grace. Ultimately, if grace is authentic in the religious sense, spiritual causation from beyond man must be operative in the "grace-full" culmination of the experience. Different patterns of causation will be operative for different individuals.

2.   *The Problem of Essential Classification*

The other problem requiring discussion at some length is whether there is a broader essence of the ENG experience. By this statement is meant the question of whether the experience is properly subsumed under some wider type of human experience which illuminates more completely its characteristics. Is there a more general mode of experience of which this part is a species? Interpretations of Hopkins often fail in this respect, it seems to me, by concentrating on some accidental classification, that is, some accidental property which may be present in the experience but which is not very illuminating because the experience would still be what it is even if that property were absent. We must ask whether there is any essential property of a wider sort that is *always* present and without which the experience would not be what it is. Only then would there be a genuine formal explanation.

Such interpretations can be grouped into two kinds: those that place the ENG experience into a broader class of nonreligious experiences and those that place it in a broader class of religious experiences. I cannot claim to deal with all possible varieties of each kind; but I shall deal with some examples of each which are illustrative and which have been prominent in the literature on Hopkins. The difficulties found in these are typical pitfalls. I shall then suggest a simpler, and I believe more accurate, way of classification.

First, an examination of nonreligious classifications is in order. Of these classifications I shall consider three that advance perhaps in subtlety but still have the common ground of subsuming the experience Hopkins portrays under a secular, psychological category.

I call the first nonreligious classification the "Jesuit Frustration Theory." According to this theory, Hopkins was a deprived victim of the repressiveness of the Jesuit order. This view is applied in the first instance to his limited poetic output and his artistry. It holds "that Hopkins's membership of the Society of Jesus was a disaster for him as a poet."[13] Literary critics have frequently clashed over the theory at this level, often called the priest-poet debate. It is as old as Charles Luxmoor's obituary letter quoted in the previous chapter[14] (though one must remember that Luxmoor recognized Hopkins's spiritual triumph none the less). "Charles Luxmoor... must be counted among the first to express the view that the Jesuit somehow crippled the artist."[15]

But the theory can be generalized to cover Hopkins's later life as a whole and hence the religious experience he articulates, which is our interest here. Instead of being a healthy-minded, joyous, thankful worshiper of God, he was, according to this account, a depressed, frustrated, wearied spiritual slave. "Hopkins suffered from infirm health, an excessively acute conscience, deep guilt complexes, and a strong, intro-punative complex aggravated by Catholicism and the priesthood."[16] John Pick, in an early article quotes John Gould Fletcher as expressing a view of this sort, which could easily be taken to refer to both art and religion: "The question however still arises whether the strict orthodoxy of the Jesuit discipline may not have somewhat limited Hopkins' mind, and whether some doctrine, capable of a broader and more personal interpretation, could not better serve the turn of those who wish today to be marked as his followers."[17] When this view is generalized to describe the ENG experience, whatever may be true of Hopkins himself, it seems to suggest that this experience is a kind of institutional oppression or at least disciplinary frustration.

Such a generalization immediately suggests the limited scope of this kind of theory. There are numerous people who can identify with Hopkins's religious experience but who have nothing to do with religious orders or disciplinary regimen. The biographical circumstance of a poet does not itself invade all of the experiences which he is able to poeticize in essence. Further, the theory would at best classify only the first phase of the experience. As far as Hopkins's own life is concerned, much has already been written to dissolve such an interpretation—not of course to deny the frustrations but to deny the Jesuit source of them. Father Martin Carroll framed this sort of denial in an earlier essay in the forties,[18] and Father Alfred Thomas has done so in a longer work more recently.[19] The plain empirical truth seems to be that "History is replete with people who have been members of a religious order and at the same time been competent, even brilliant, successes in the major walks of life. Our expectations of true religion lead us to think of vocational enhancement rather than the inhibitions of honorable human endeavors."[20]

The second nonreligious classification can be called the "Chronic Self-pity Theory." If the experience to which Hopkins gives expression is not that of "a genius blasted by asceticism,"[21] rooted in disciplinary regimen, is there perhaps some emotional category that would comprise it? One theory of this sort is that the experience is not a genuine religious experience but a kind of self-indulgent absorption in one's own feelings. The theory may be introduced by some words of F.R. Leavis, which are made, however, oddly enough, not in reference to Hopkins but in reference to a portion of Eliot's *Ash Wednesday*. Leavis does not hold this view about Hopkins; but his remarks will be useful to indicate a possible category of interpretation.

> It seems to me that here his heroic wrestling to discover what he is and what and how he believes has lapsed into self-deception. It is not conscious insincerity: that isn't the dangerous kind. But he has yielded to the insidious temptation his inner disunity exposes him to: he takes for the achieved clear-eyed humility of complete and sure self-knowledge what is not that.[22]

The type of self-delusion here mentioned would probably not be attributed to Hopkins with his frequent searching and darkened states. But some type of self-delusion might well be. The self-delusion involved might be alleged to be that of taking as religious purgation and illumination what is only effusive, even adolescent, self-pity.

Yvor Winters's well-known view of Hopkins can be appropriated to illustrate such an interpretation. He rejects the Jesuit frustration theory; but he does interpret Hopkins, the poet, as a romanticist and emotionalist. This interpretation might well be extended to mean that the religious sentiment in the poetry shares in the general emotive tone of the poetry, which Winters takes often to be that of self-pity and hypocrisy. He admits only five outstanding poems in the entire canon as judged by his intellectualist theory of poetry. "The most nearly successful poems," he says, "are the following: *The Habit of Perfection, The Valley of the Elwy, Inversnaid, St. Alphonsus Rodriguez,* and *To him who ever thought with Love of me.*"[23] For the most part the rest come under his strictures against emotive sentimentality in poetry. One key passage is this:

> I believe that Hopkins is a poet who will find his most devout admirers among the young.... They are likely to be somewhat emotional and hence uncritical of emotion in others; they are likely to be given to self-pity at odd moments, and hence sympathetic with chronic self-pity in others. I am not one of those who find failure more impressive than success, though I realize that I am in a minority.[24]

This view is, I believe, a most provocative theory and not itself an adolescent one, as some might contend. The reason is that most people know all too well the human tendency to self-deception. How easy it is to take one's own strong pathos, one's own ego-preoccupation to be an indicator of some profound meaning, some great insight, some dazzling truth, even some mandated destiny, when all one is doing is (to speak like an adolescent) kidding himself. Self-pity becomes noble glory through easy psychic chicanery. How jarring would it then be to be called out of one's swoon by hearing someone say: "One is inclined to ask: 'What do you know of these matters? Why are you so secretive? And above all, why are you so self-righteous in your secretiveness?'"[25]

Now it will not be enough merely to deny flatly that this is what Hopkins was doing, for that would not answer a charge of rationalization. But one can counter with this: the ENG experience that Hopkins depicts is not simply emotion. There is also action in it. The action comes mainly in the second phase, naturation, where one is willfully moving and struggling to extricate oneself. An emotionalist classification cannot, therefore, be adequate. Then one can also say that if someone has reached the point of making a serious commitment to himself to undertake deliberate, concerted action to extricate himself, it is reasonable to suppose that one was in a genuine state of barrenness and desolation and not merely a self-deluding facsimile of this state. Self-deceptions seem to call forth not commitment of effort but prolongation of self-indulgent brooding. Then too, if grace is a real possibility in one's scheme, it would require an openness to receive from without rather than an emotive closure within. I do not mean to say there could be no experiences appearing to be like the genuine one but which are in fact self-delusions, blustery fakes, but only to say there is no reason to think the ENG experience has this property essentially.

The last nonreligious classification I call the "Yoke of Transcendence Theory." The last theory in this group holds that the essence of the experience lies not in the disciplinary regimen by itself, or even in religion as such, but in that specific kind of religion (and this description would apply to most religions indeed) which appeals to transcendent reality and not to earth alone. A strident spokesman for this approach is Theodore Weiss. He sees Hopkins's religious life as divided into two stages. In Hopkins's earlier poetic career Hopkins had a closeness to nature—sensuous, earthy, immanent—a religion of earth. Then he fell into transcendent religion and everything went bad. The later poetry shows unconquered despair rooted in the religious shift.

Weiss's basic premise is that the artistic spirit, and presumably the human spirit generally, is liberated when it is united with sensuous nature, bringing an immanent accord of spirit and earth. There is, he admits, a "seeming conflict between spirit and earth"; but it is possible to overcome this conflict, and in fact there has been a "reconciliation and happy marriage eventually consummated by the larger artists,... who, deriving their spirit-strength and substance from the earth, in the end proved the two identical."[26] Hopkins at first had this spirit, Weiss suggests, and was a sensuous poet of nature religion. Attempting a poem of his own about Hopkins, Weiss depicts this early Hopkins as follows:

> ... the vast and healthy humanity in him
> as richly rooted to the earth

as the finest most delicate flower
or the tiny glistening blade of grass—
he fire refined to its most human essential
singing of the sensuality of the spirit
and the spirit of sensuality
he as earthly-divine
as the bird's wing and its feathered throat.[27]

But this early spirit of Hopkins is said to have faded, so that Hopkins "gradually discovered himself falling into the abyss, widening steadily, between religion and actuality."[28] The reader is then told that "Hopkins soon learned how inadequate religion was for him" and that he became a victim of "religion's refusal to free him to the infinite delights of this world."[29] As a final estimate of the later period, from which I have drawn heavily for my account of the ENG experience, Weiss asserts the following:

> Denied, starved, Hopkins's senses waned. Religion and the earth, no longer synonymous for him, in his last years he could not accept the realizations living, with ever more urgent cogency, thrust upon him. Certainly he could no longer reconcile them to his life, religion. ... Bent to the yoke of the cross for some twenty years, he could no longer either drop it or carry it.[30]

As a preliminary refutation of Weiss's view, it may be remarked first that the division of Hopkins's career into two parts, one of sensuous immanence and one of yoked transcendence, is indefensible. It is in fact extraordinarily naive. No one converts from Anglicanism to Catholicism and then enters the Jesuit order without a serious commitment to a transcendent deity. Hopkins's religion embraced transcendence from the beginning and throughout his life. His love of nature was not his religion but his appreciation of the transcendent God's immanent activity. Moreover, as I have documented already, especially in chapters four and five, his crisis in later years was not one of radical doubt in transcendent religion: he did not suffer from belief in transcendent grace but acknowledged it as the source of such consolation as he had. "He seems never to have undergone a crisis in faith similar to those chronicled in *In Memoriam* or *Dover Beach*."[31] Furthermore, the claim that Hopkins lost his sensuous delight in nature seems to be factually false. Patricia Ball in a recent work includes a letter of Hopkins which she calls "An Unpublished Letter from Hopkins to Nature."[32] It is from the Dublin period, Hopkins's worst stage, and yet it is filled with the minute sensory descriptions characteristic of his early diaries and poems. It deals mainly with the color effects around the sun which stem from the sun's halo or corona. It is vivid and concrete in description, though Hopkins's interest by this time is more mixed with scientific interests, as might be expected.

But this general theory could be held without these peculiar views about Hopkins himself. Therefore, the approach of J. Hillis Miller, which belongs in the same category, is far more respectable. His interpretation is vastly more subtle, less given to superficial over-simplifications, and far more sensitive to both the poetical and the religious nuances in Hopkins's total work.

I cannot go into the detailed organization of Hopkins's poetic life which Miller gives in his perceptive essay on Hopkins in *The Disappearance of God*. That account centers on a threefold development in the concept of inscape and focuses on the self, nature, and Christ. This account is of great interest in its own right, and at times it offers a reading rather close to the presentation I have made in previous chapters. For example, grace is not ignored. Miller can write, at one point: "No one has expressed more powerfully than Hopkins the sense of an internal hemorrhage of the soul, an innate propensity of the self to fall in on itself and disappear. Only the perpetually renewed gift of creative grace can counteract this dia-bolical gravity of the soul".[33]

But in the end this fuller description is only of psychological value in Hopkins and is ontologically unfounded, according to Miller. What stands out in the end as the essence of the experience is the disappearance of God, with the renewals of nature and of God being merely pious hopes without fulfillment. Hopkins's life closes with no God and only wishful thinking that things might be better beyond the grave.

Hopkins, who seems so different from other nineteenth-century writers who suffered the absence of God, in reality ends in a similar place. Like so many of his contemporaries, he believes in God, but is unable to reach him. Deserted by his nature, he is left with a blind violence of will toward a God who keeps himself absent. The saving power can come, for him at least, only beyond the gates of death.[34]

The reason for this futile end clearly is, according to Miller, transcendental religion. A recovery would have been possible through a return to earth, a humanistic settling. But it was not found by Hopkins. Miller's final summation is this:

> Only in Browning, of the writers studied here, are there hints and anticipations of that recovery of immanence which was to be the inner drama of twentieth-century literature. Browning alone seems to have glimpsed the fact that the sad alternatives of nihilism and escape beyond the world could be evaded if man would only reject twenty-five hundred years of belief in the dualism of heaven and earth. If man could do this he might come to see that being and value lie in this world, in what is immanent, tangible, present to man.... But Browning, like De Quincey, Arnold, Hopkins, and Emily Brontë, was stretched on the rack of a fading transcendental-ism.[35]

The view of Miller's volume, or at least a view based upon it, appears to come to this: God as a transcendent being does not exist or at least cannot be known; since transcendental religion therefore is false, it cannot possibly provide a means of recovery that is grounded in reality rather than illusion. Hence the disappearance of God must be a dominant feature of the ENG experience and the rest of it mostly self-deception or wishful thinking.

Such a view brings this study, of course, directly to the point at which theological faiths conflict and personal decisions are made. One can ask, furthermore, whether this handling of the phenomenology is even psychologically correct in Hopkins's case. It seems to me that the evidence from the letters and the poems simply does not support the contention that the disappearance of God coupled with wishful thinking is the last word in the Hopkins story. The recoveries of naturation and grace seem as stabilizing and as profound as the elements of encagement are distressing. And if this conception of experience is true in Hopkins, there is no reason to think it could not be true in many other persons who undergo the ENG experience. To be sure, one could say that it is impossible because transcendental religion is false. Yet one ought, I suppose, to study the facts themselves and not be content merely to deduce empirical psychological facts from theological or anti-theological dogmas.

Having examined nonreligious classifications, I would like to turn now to some views that classify the ENG experience under some religious category of explanation. I shall limit the discussion of religious interpretations to three of the common possibilities.

Category one is referred to as "Devotionalism." Perhaps the simplest of all classifications looks on Hopkins's poetry as nothing more or less than devotional utterance. This flat statement would mean the experience that this study is concerned with is a simple devotional experience. The first book on Hopkins, which was written by Elizabeth Phare in 1933, seems to take something like this simplistic approach. She divides Hopkins's religious poetry into didactic verse and devotional verse, and the poems with which this study is mainly concerned, including the desolation poems, come in the devotional category.[36] She rightly objects to I. A. Richards's calling the desolation poems "poems of doubt."[37] But is there much advance in merely calling them devotional? A possible definition of this category appears when Miss Phare speaks of the devotional poems as being "the poems which deal with Hopkins' experience as an individual soul rather than as one of the many members of the Christian Church."[38] Devotional poetry would thus be the private, subjective effusings of a poet in relation to God, which effusings presumably would be designed to prompt similar meditations in others.

One might note in passing that if the poems were really so private in this sense, it would be difficult to see them as rendering a more universal experience as we have done. And in fact this subjective view seems to be contradicted by Miss Phare's own conclusion when she says at the end: "Hopkins in his best work comes as near as, say, Dante, to making his experience available to all."[39]

But the main point to make is that the classification is too incomplete. The term "devotional" may suggest more of the positive spiritual outcome characteristic of the last part of the experience than the full scope of the experience. Thus, while the previous theories tend to focus exclusively on the desolation phase, this theory focuses too much on the final phase. Also "devotion" suggests more of inspiration and meditation than is fitting, and hence may be misleading. It is true that one should not think of devotional poetry as limited to easy spirituality or cheap, mundane inspiration. The stark and the deep are also stimulants to meditation and religious awareness. But then all of this consideration is perhaps not captured best by the term "devotional."

The second religious explanatory category can be referred to as "Didactic Christian Witness." Equally simplistic is the view that would classify Hopkins's religious poetry as straightforward instruction in Christian truth. Father Robert Boyle, an expert on Hopkins, tends to speak in this vein. For example, he encourages the teaching of Hopkins's poetry for this purpose. He says that "it would advance the glory of God as the study of no other body of poetry would do, because it would lead them to the realization that all this beauty is but a faint reflection of the beauty of God." And he continues with clearly didactic intent: "It is no small thing that we have the truths of our faith in artistic form."[40] One consequence of this view may be to disregard the reality of the suffering, the desolation, and the emptiness in the experience. Since the poetry is seen as a teaching mirror of doctrinal truth, its personal anguish and triumph are only vehicles. Thus Father Lahey can write: "The celebrated 'terrible' sonnets are only terrible in the same way that the beauty of Jesus Christ is terrible. Only the strong pinions of an eagle can realize the cherished happiness of such suffering. ... Read in this light his poems cease to be tragic."[41]

Of course one must acknowledge that the appreciator of these poems will find them insightful, provocative, and in some Socratic way instructional. But their primary impact in this regard is not likely to be doctrinal or didactic, the presentation of "the truths of our faith" in beautiful form. To speak doctrinally too quickly in this manner is to substitute abstractions for the personal experiential character of the ENG experience.[42] And in this connection one may note Abbott's comments on Lahey's view of the later sonnets. "Their evidence," Abbott says, "and the evidence of the letters, is directly contrary"[43] (contrary to Lahey's view). Abbott focuses on the personal import of these poems of Hopkins:

> These poems are salt with the taste of his blood and bitter with the
> sweat of his anguish, the work of a man tried to the utmost limit

of his strength and clinging to the last ledge where reason may find
a refuge. Their authority and truthfulness cannot be questioned.
Here, indeed, is a chart of despair, made by one who still believes
in the justice of God.[44]

And if the account has a generality for others, it is this felt experience
that is essential, with doctrinal articulation coming as an aftermath.

The last religious category of explanation I shall deal with in
this study is "Mysticism." One of the most common religious interpretations of Hopkins, especially among various Catholic writers,
has held that he belongs in the mystical tradition. Sometimes this
interpretation is taken to mean that he exemplifies specifically the
classical pattern of the purgative way, the illuminative way, and the
mystical way. Sometimes it is a more loosely defined claim that he
somehow discloses that spiritual communion with God characteristic
of mysticism. The first writer to have advanced this mystical interpretation seems to be Father Lahey, who sees Hopkins going through
the "dark night of the soul," a stage just prior to final rapturous
union. Speaking of Hopkins's final sorrow, Lahey says:

> It sprang from causes which have their origin in true mysticism.
> Hopkins, smiling and joyful with his friends, was at the same time
> on the bleak heights of spiritual night with his God. All writers on
> mysticism... have told us that this severe trial is the greatest and
> most cherished *gift* from One Who has accepted literally His servant's
> oblation.[45]

Another priest, E. K. Taylor, says of the Dublin poems that "the full
depth of their meaning can only be appreciated in the light of
mystical theology," and that "the state of mind evinced by these
poems would seem to have much in common with that of a soul
experiencing the Dark Night of the Senses."[46] Still another explicit
identification of Hopkins with mysticism is made in the following
quotation:

> Yet he is a poet most deserving of the name in its true meaning.
> Mysticism, in the Catholic sense, means a union, during this life,
> of the soul with God in sublime contemplation; so intimate that
> the soul well-nigh loses itself in its transformation into God. ...
> From his poems, it appears that Hopkins experienced these tests,

and so was admitted to this close, contemplative union with his God.[47]

And the account can become even more lyrical in its description: "Hopkins passed successfully through these dark nights, and his soul seems to mount triumphantly to that state, the mystical state of spiritual marriage.... Briefly, Gerard Manley Hopkins deserves to be numbered with England's great mystics."[48]

One wonders at the outset which poems and letters such writers have in mind in claiming that they exhibit a spiritual union "so intimate that the soul well-nigh loses itself in its transformation into God." There are certainly signs of recovery from grief, testimonies to grace-given renewal, and indications that Hopkins's life ended in a happy state. But all this seems quite different from mystical union. I am bound to agree with Andreach's conclusion: "If a mystic is one who experiences infused contemplation... and a mystical poet is one who translates this experience into poetry, then Hopkins is not a mystical poet."[49] One is tempted to think that this theory is based not so much on direct evidence as upon an extrapolated inference about the poetry. This inference might be posited as follows: The poems express desolation, and it is hard to believe this desolation is real in the literal sense. It is too desperate, too vivid, to be fully real. It must be phenomenal only, masking some ulterior meaning. The phenomenon of mysticism lies ready to hand for interpretation. So the desolation must actually be the "dark night" phase; and if that is present then the final culmination has to be there also, and so Hopkins is a mystic. But such an extrapolation does not seem to fit the facts of the poems and letters.

I have come down hard on those nonreligious interpretations which have concentrated on the bleak desolation and ignored the real signs of religious recovery and renewal. But I must also demur from those religious interpretations which so elevate the spiritual triumph as to minimize the real, living, personal character of the desolation. One cannot give a merely phenomenal reading of this phase in order to support an overdrawn spiritual interpretation.

I quote below a passage from Evelyn Underhill recounting the onset of the mystic "dark night," and this quotation will show how little this "dark night" theory applies to Hopkins. The "dark night" is viewed as a fatigue reaction to a previous state of pure illumination and perfect contentment, a state with which Hopkins seems never to have been blessed during his lifetime, as we have seen in chapter five. His was a running and very human mundane mixture of decline and ascent in felt consolation. Underhill writes:

> During the time in which the illuminated consciousness is fully established, the self, as a rule, is perfectly content: believing that in its vision of eternity, its intense and loving consciousness of God, it has reached the goal of its quest. Sooner or later, however, psychic fatigue sets in; the state of illumination begins to break up, the complementary negative consciousness appears, and shows itself as an overwhelming sense of darkness and deprivation. This sense is so deep and strong that it inhibits all consciousness of the Transcendent; and plunges the self into the state of negation and misery which is called the Dark Night. ... Psychologically considered, the Dark Night is an example of the operation of the law of reaction from stress. It is a period of fatigue and lassitude following a period of sustained mystical activity.[50]

Some of the descriptive phrases that do not seem to pertain to Hopkins are: "the illuminated consciousness is fully established," "perfectly content," "reached the goal of its quest," "inhibits all consciousness of the Transcendent," and "a period of sustained mystical activity." Further, although some of the phrases describing the "dark night" would be similar to those describing Hopkins's encagement, a different connotation would be involved if they were understood not as existential problems but as a temporary letdown within a mystical crescendo. Finally, the phrases used later to intimate the ultimate state of the unitive life, following the "dark night" stage, seem equally inapplicable to Hopkins; for example, "final triumph of the spirit," "the flower of mysticism," "humanity's top note," "the consummation," "living at transcendent levels of reality," "breathing an atmosphere whose true quality we cannot even conceive," and "utter transmutation of the self in God."[51]

Even if Hopkins should turn out to have been a mystic in the sense these writers have in mind, the experience generalized here from the poems and letters would still not be of that sort. And since my interest is not biographical but phenomenological, little would be altered. Such a discrepancy would, however, be surprising, to say the least. On the whole, it seems best to leave this possibility aside also, even in the limited version suggested by Andreach, who, in his reading of Hopkins, keeps the purgative way and the illuminative way and omits only the unitive way.[52] It is the general classification itself that is misleading.

As a result of the above rejection of so many unsatisfactory attempts to classify the ENG experience under either a wider nonreligious category or a wider religious category, one must conclude that the best way to view the experience is as a distinctive type of religious experience in its own right. It is not readily subsumable under other familiar types of religious experience, such as conversion or mysticism or worship or meditation or faithful service. The all-encompassing category of religious life is man's emotional, volitional, and intellectual relation to the ultimate being, and the ENG experience is certainly a part of that human religious pilgrimage. But it is a distinctive part, not essentially the same as other experiences. It is that phase of a postconversion or postcommitment life in which, though serving as one is able and seeking sanctification, one nevertheless, for one reason or another, encounters encagement with all its pangs but still is faith-filled, still finds some resources for recovery at one's disposal, and still receives the joyful restoration attributed to divine mercy. There seems nothing quite like this as a religious experience.

It is possible to bring the ENG experience under a broader category that is neither religious nor nonreligious in itself but could become either—the category of desolation and recovery. Such a description could apply in secular contexts like psychotherapy or artistic creativity or just a lapse and renewal in ordinary life. It can also have religious meaning, as I have already outlined. Such a classification would be useful for general communication if all I wanted to do was convey in general what I am studying, namely, the ENG experience as dealing with personal desolation and recovery. But this classification in no way "explains" the nature of the experience; it merely helps to locate it. It is like saying that American presidents belong in the class of national executives, which class includes both Americans and non-Americans. This categorization may be useful but does not go very far to characterize the office of the American president. It only marks off in general what one is examining.

Another general classification is possible within the religious sphere. Frederick Streng, for example, has distinguished four ways of being religious, which he calls "personal apprehension of the holy," "sacred action: myth and sacrament," "harmony with cosmic law," and "freedom through spiritual insight" (mysticism).[53] In this classification the ENG experience would come under the first grouping, "personal apprehension of the holy," and more particularly the personalistic-theistic part of this way. It is an experience in the life of individual persons in their confrontation with the holy "other" or God. But this too is a general historic rubric and tells us nothing about the specific character of the ENG experience. I have assumed that the frame of reference for Hopkins's account is personal theism and more particularly Christian theism. My question was what is the nature of the specific kind of experience he expresses within this frame of reference. So again the classification is useful as a marker but is not a complete explanation.

I do not conclude that the ENG experience is so unique that it is not open to any broader classifications of this sort. Not at all. Most things can be classified in countless ways. What I have argued against in the polemics of this chapter is certain claims that this *specific kind* of experience is virtually identical with some other *specific kind* of experience, religious or nonreligious. Such identity-imputing classifications seem to me not to work out. And it is for this reason that the distinctiveness of the experience is being emphasized. But from another viewpoint, with different purposes, one could also say that the experience is, after all, part of human religiousness in various ways.

3.   The Problem of Purpose

I said earlier that the function or purpose that the ENG experience might be conceived to have would depend on one's theological outlook. From a naturalistic standpoint the experience would be seen as serving at best a moral strengthening function but more probably an enervating function—because human energy would be deflected away from important humanistic goals into a supernatural concern. From a theological standpoint, on the other hand, the question of what purposes might be divinely intended becomes meaningful. This theological question in turn can be usefully divided into two forms: first, what specific aims does God have for specific individuals in bringing about the specific experiences that they undergo; and second, what general ends does God prevision for the ENG experience in creating a world in which such experience is a possibility?

The first question is the more individual, personal one. It could only be answered and studied case by case. It carries the suggestion that God has deliberately sent the experience (or arranged the experience) so as to accomplish some specific result in an individual's life. When overdrawn, this view runs the risk of obliterating any freedom or indeterminism in the world which one may also wish to champion, even as a theological tenet. Nevertheless, the record of religious testimonials is replete with readings of this kind. Analyzing their own experiences, people may say things like: "God must have wanted me to do this," "God was trying to show me something," "God must not have wanted me to go in that direction," "God was leading me in his own way," "I was shaken out of my downhill course," "God was teaching me what such-and-such means," and so on. To give a compilation and analysis of such teleological readings would constitute a phenomenological study in itself. The common assumption here probably is that freedom is not being negated but that God is nonetheless sufficiently active in the experience to cause formidable options to appear for the person's decision.

The second question is an easier one for generalizing, though none the easier theologically. It seems to me that if one sticks to Hopkins's own reading without venturing into theology systematically, there are two principal purposes of the ENG experience which he affirms. There is also a third which is very much in accord with his philosophy but not very prominent in his writing as an explicit final cause of this type of experience. Paradoxically enough, I find a good statement of it in J. Hillis Miller, who has been criticized previously in this chapter but who makes an interesting observation for the present context.

The first of these purposes is that of bringing a person into a more perfect communion, dialogue, or relationship with God. Whatever the precise elements of the experience in an individual case are, its possibility of occurrence is seen as a possible avenue to effect this divine-human cognition. For some it may be seen as a means to this end which would not have been reached, or would not be so likely to have been reached, in any other way.

The second purpose Hopkins sees is the strengthening of the will. Through this strengthening the weak will is fortified and amplified. The hardhearted will is mellowed and changed. This effect would include the moral will, or the will in its moral function, but also the will in its other functions, religious or secular.

The third purpose is that of divine encouragement to a person to be a genuine individual. That is, one is pressured in the direction of completing the fulfillment of one's unique individuality rather than allowed to sink into oblivion of self. Miller states this possibility as follows: "Having created the self, God holds it at arm's length and forces it to persist in its own likeness to him."[54] That is, God as a unique being has created other unique selves to *be* other unique selves in their full finite perfection, and he must sometimes jar them severely into this. Their tendency to give up or to lose self in submission and abnegation, even if this loss of self is of a religious character, cannot be tolerated. The initial phase of the experience may indeed be felt with dread by the self, as if it were being "held poised over a nothingness by a divine 'pressure'"; but God is always present and "acts directly on the soul in every moment of its existence" in order to further genuine selfhood.[55]

There is perhaps a relationship between these three purposes and the three phases of the ENG experience itself. Communion with God seems the special outcome of grace; strengthening of will seems particularly related to naturation; and individuality may seem the special outcome of the desolation-isolation syndrome. One should not push this division very far, however, since theologically one would undoubtedly wish to say that one is considering here a total experience whose possibility as a totality might have all of these purposes as its joint final cause. In any case the three purposes, even if only loosely linked to the three phases, have an ordering in priority which is the reverse of that which was followed in this study in the earlier phenomenology of phases. There the movement from encagement through naturation through grace was followed, which progression suggests an ascending scale in religious movement and often a chronological sequence as well. But of the purposes mentioned here, the priority would be communion with God, then strengthening of man's will to do work in the world, then the achievement of each person's full individuality. One is almost tempted to say that these three theological purposes are in a way spiritual, moral, and artistic; and that of these the spiritual is paramount, the moral next essential, and the artistic complementary in the total design.

CHAPTER VII

Hopkins's Philosophy
of Religion

HAVING DEALT in previous chapters with a religious phenomenology and its interpretation, I wish to inquire now about the framework of religious thought in Hopkins which lies behind his expression of this experience. What is the philosophy of religion in Hopkins's thinking?

It might be said that there is no such thing: Hopkins was a loyal Catholic, and Catholicism provided the background he had. At most, one could speak of his Ignatian world-view, as Downes does.[1] But this general world view does not mean that no individual distinctiveness remains. Neither the comprehensiveness of dogma nor the regimen of discipline is so all-pervasive that it rules out particular emphases, special interests, personal directions, favored nuances, and explanatory ventures of thought. Were this fact not so, all men would be general forms rather than individual creatures. In fact, however, there is good philosophical reason in Scotus's notion of *haecceitas*, which Hopkins accepted, to look for the individualized character of a person's thought in addition to his orthodoxy. Therefore Gardner perhaps gives the reader the wrong impression when he says of Hopkins: "Boldly independent in Art and Metaphysics, he was always, in Religion, the humble child of Authority."[2] Hopkins fully obeyed authority; but such obedience is not incompatible with active thinking about religion and God. Nor are dogma and discipline intended to supply answers to all philosophical questions, even about religion. There does seem to be adequate room, then, for investigating Hopkins's pattern of religious thought.

Still one might say that, even if this much were to be granted, Hopkins put small emphasis on philosophy; he was a priest and poet; therefore one might conclude that there is not enough to go on for such a project. Now even if this analysis were so, it need not deflect this project; for it might be possible to ferret out from a writer an implicit philosophy of religion just as it was possible to identify a phenomenology of religious experience implicit in Hopkins's poetry. As a matter of fact, however, his own testimony testifies to his great concern with philosophical matters. In one sense these interests rank higher than his poetic interests in his rational ordering of priorities, whatever his feelings might have been. He writes as follows in a letter to Canon Dixon as late as 1887:

> What becomes of my verses I care little, but about things like this, what I write or could write on philosophical matters, I do; and the reason of the difference is that the verses stand or fall by their simple selves and, though by being read they might do good, by being unread they do no harm; but if the other things are unsaid right they will be said by somebody else wrong, and that is what will not let me rest.[3]

Thus having an image of Hopkins as an authority-bound priest doing poetry on the sly simply will not do. He was zealously concerned with philosophical matters, though it is true there is little overt proof of his concern to go on. His remaining philosophical material is scattered and in fragments. I shall seek to draw upon such little pieces, as well as general allusions, to present a sketch of the individually distinctive themes in Hopkins's religious thought. In this sketch I shall assume, not reject, that his Catholicism was orthodox and his Ignatian loyalty complete. The point is that there simply is more, much more, to say.

Since I am calling this project philosophy of religion, it is important to clarify the use of the terms "religion" and "philosophy of religion" inasmuch as I am using these in somewhat more restricted senses than is customary. The term "religion" is commonly used to cover a vast array of cultural phenomena—beliefs and creeds, ex-

periences and attitudes, institutions and practices of many sorts. I
shall be focusing, however, on religion considered as a personal disposition, roughly captured in the phrase "being religious." Vernon J.
Bourke has a helpful definition of this signification: "Religion is a
special virtue of the human will, perfecting the moral agent and his
actions, in order that he may give to God the honor, which is owed
to Him."[4] To speak of religion as a virtue is not to make it a subjective feeling, a private glow, for the reference to God is part of the
definition. Nor are external acts repudiated, for the perfecting of
religion takes place in the agent *and* his actions.

This study intends to survey, then, Hopkins's reflective views that
are related in some way, doctrinally or practically, to this virtue of
religion or the state of personal religiousness. And these reflective
views I shall call his philosophy of religion.

Much else is usually included in the philosophy of religion. Today
there is great emphasis on the logical and the linguistic analyses of
religious concepts. Yet some philosophers are reacting against this
trend and are moving in a direction more akin to the above notion
in which philosophers reflect on actual human religiousness and not
just on abstract concepts. Louis Dupré, for instance, writing in the
International Philosophical Quarterly, writes:

> Much of what is written in the philosophy of religion deals with
> abstract generalities and makes exceedingly tedious reading. It is
> as if philosophers had not yet learned to apply to religion what they
> do as a matter of course in the area of science: to acquaint them-
> selves thoroughly with the subject. ... What we need, far more than
> the current analysis of presumably universal concepts, is a philoso-
> phical equivalent of Bremond's *Histoire littéraire du sentiment
> religieux.*[5]

In giving limited endorsement to this view for the present occasion,
I do not mean to exclude the analytic approach from the philosophy
of religion. In other contexts, it would be appropriate to undertake
the logical analysis of religious concepts. It is just that in the present
case things stand differently. There are many mansions in the philosophy of religion with different suitable approaches.

I believe that the "religious aspect of philosophy," in Royce's
phrase, was what chiefly interested Hopkins about philosophy, and

this fact too would accord with our restriction of the subject. I do not mean that religious philosophy is the only important part of philosophy, even in Hopkins's own view of philosophy, but only that it is his special concern. Hopkins had a more than ordinary passion for religion, even for a religious devotee. "Religion, you know," he writes to his friend Baillie, "enters very deep; in reality it is the deepest impression I have in speaking to people, that they are or that they are not of my religion."[6] In this connection, having quoted Gardner somewhat adversely before, I quote him more sympathetically here: "Moreover, the impassioned observations in the Journals increase our understanding not only of the imagination which could turn to Sprung Rhythm and other new verse-modes, but also of the intellect which turned to religion for philosophic assurance."[7] To turn to religion for philosophic assurance is not to imply that religion is a replacement for philosophy, as if philosophy were a lower rival on the same plane. Religion, after all, is a virtue of the will, philosophy of the intellect. It only means that philosophy for Hopkins had to be worked out in coordination with religious sentiment and that religion provides the special clues for answering philosophical questions, at least those which most interested him.

There are two general points about Hopkins's view of religion which I should like to stress before attempting a more systematic account. One is that the concern for objective truth is essential to an adequate religious understanding. The other is that religion is an intensely practical demand and not merely a stimulus to intellectualizing. To hold these two points together might seem paradoxical. Yet the classical Christian tradition sees them as mutually supportive: if religion is ultimately a demand, it is vital that it be directed toward truth; and if there is objective religious truth in its own right, it is vital that we desire its appropriation.

There is a tendency in some quarters to see all religion as mythology, neither true nor false but only symbolical in some sense, and then to judge it entirely from its pragmatic value or cultural value. Hopkins has little patience with such a view. Religion loses its urgency if it is merely psychological play-acting and not devoted to what is deemed true in an objective sense. Religion must be judged in this light. This view is clear from a letter to Dixon in which Hopkins is commenting on mythology: "But mythology is something else besides fairytale: it is religion, the historical part of religion. ...

And could I speak too severely of it? First it is as history untrue. What is untrue history? Nothing and worse than nothing. And that history religion? Still worse.''[8] These are strong words, but they illustrate the uncompromising place that Hopkins gives to the concern for truth in religion. This devotion to truth could lead to great complexity and subtlety of an intellectual kind; and while Hopkins was not a philosophical theologian, there are passages in his prose which move in this direction. Such work may be necessary because once one has committed oneself to truth, argument and implication must be followed through, as Socrates taught us.

At the same time intellectuality is not what religion is all about. The final religious aim is to be in a religious state honoring God, to perfect the virtue of religion. This statement means that religion could have an utter simplicity about it also; and Hopkins was a master, both in poetry and in prose, at illuminating its character with brilliant simplicity. As a sample and archetype of this mastery, I choose two lines from his unfinished poem, "St. Thecla." He has Thecla sitting near St. Paul and listening to his preaching:

> He spoke of God the Father and His Son,
> Of world made, marred, and mended, lost and won.
> *(Poems, no. 136)*

These lines may be taken as an utterly simple statement of what the Christian religion at least is all about: God creator and Christ redeemer, world divinely made, humanly marred, and jointly (though mainly by grace) mended. Never are the simple, central, essential demands to be lost sight of in favor of unfruitful bypaths that tempt the mind.

Truth and practicality, with their attendant complexity and simplicity, thus characterize the religious quest. They will be understood as background as this study progresses.

In what follows I shall be moving in a sense from relatively more practical to relatively more theoretical aspects of Hopkins's thinking about religion. There will not be a total separation, however, either chronologically or qualitatively, in the various sections. The discussion will begin with what is practically central in religion—religion as demand and norm for living—and will then gradually move to topics where theory is uppermost.

1. The Single and Ultimate End

Following Ignatius, biblical teaching, and Christian tradition generally, Hopkins insists uncompromisingly that the single and ultimate end of man's being is to praise and serve God. There is nothing new in this idea, but it is essential. This belief is the simple norm that lies behind all religion: God is the goal of life. Every aspect of life must be directed to this end. Hopkins never deviates from this commitment and total demand; as Gardner sums up the idea, "Religion, for him, was the total reaction of the whole man to the whole of life. Man was created to praise and serve God."[9]

Here is a typical statement by Hopkins himself on this point, given in an 1879 sermon at St. Joseph's Church in Bedford Leigh: "This is the purpose of the world, the end of our being: when we have once said from our hearts/Glory be to God/we have answered the end of our being, we have born fruit to our maker, we have made it worth his while to create us, we have not lived in vain."[10]

The very purpose in creation, according to Hopkins, is to set forth a domain that magnifies God:

> Why Did God Create?—Not for sport, not for nothing. ... He meant the world to give him praise, reverence, and service; *to give him glory*. ... It is a book he has written, of the riches of his knowledge, teaching endless truths, full lessons of wisdom, a poem of beauty; what is it about? His praise, the reverence due to him, the way to serve him; it tells him of his glory.
>
> (*Sermons*, 238-9)

But why should one accept this glorification of God as his life's goal? As free agents people are capable of not doing so. Consequently they must be convinced and enjoined. The primary justification Hopkins seems to appeal to here is God's absolute sovereignty as creator. It is the prerogative of a creator to place the imprint of his will on the creature; and if the creature was made with the inherent purpose of glorifying God, then he is bound to do so if he is to act in a way befitting the form he has. Hopkins likes to use the image of king and subjects in stating this obligation to sovereign authority, as in this excerpt from the sermon given 4 January 1880 at St. Frances Xavier Church in Liverpool: "Who is God that he wishes our love?—there is the root of the matter. A sovereign, a lord and master, a king, a sovereign; he a sovereign, we his subjects. A sovereign asks his subjects for love" (*Sermons*, 52).

One should not read this quotation to mean, however, a mere submission to authority as power alone. God unites power with infinite goodness, and it is because of this goodness that submission is justified finally. The New Testament declares that God is love (1 John 4:8), not that he is sheer power. Moreover, divine goodness involves the communication and sharing of good with creatures to enable them to partake of the goodness of being. This sharing aspect of the divine nature is stressed in the *Spiritual Exercises,* which Hopkins followed, as the motivation for serving God:

> I will rouse myself to reckon how much our Lord God has done for me, how much that is His own He has shared with me; I will further consider the divine plan whereby this same Lord wants to give me all that it is in His power to give. I then turn to myself and try to see what reason and justice demand that I offer, nay, give, His divine majesty in return—all that belongs to me, and with it all that I am in myself—in the spirit of one who makes a present out of a great love.[11]

The individual, then, is to direct his will outward to God rather than inward to ego-preoccupation. Religion is worship of God and not a self-salvation technique. In the process, however, the individual is also brought to his own fulfillment, so one should not think of religion as obliteration of self. "Man has been created," Loyola says, "to praise, reverence, and serve our Lord God, thereby saving his soul."[12] The word "thereby" is important. Individual salvation is a consequence, an attendant result (albeit an integral one), of the primary goal.

This point is much misunderstood and maligned by those who charge Christianity with religious egoism in this regard. Yet upon reflection the charge seems misdirected; for in contemplating a perfected community—even an ideal society, let alone a kingdom of God—it would seem perverse to exclude someone solely on account of his sacrifice or altruism. Actually the moral distinction between egoism and altruism seems strangely unhelpful in understanding the final goal of religious perfection in creation. This goal is a commonweal ideally including the fulfillment of all created persons in relation to God. So at least Hopkins conceives of it, as stated simply in another of the Liverpool sermons of 18 January 1880:

> Now *what was the common weal?* what was the joint and common good of that kingdom?—it was that God should be glorified in man and man glorified in God. Man was created to praise, honor, and serve God, thus fulfilling God's desire in bringing him into being, and by so doing to save his soul, thus fulfilling his own desire, the desire of everything that has being. He was created to give God glory and by so doing to win himself glory.
>
> (Sermons, 59)

This single and ultimate end enjoins a single-minded practical course in life and shows all men what to live for in all they do. Thus "any day, any minute we bless God for our being or for anything, for food, for sunlight, we do and are what we were meant for, made for—things that give and mean to give God glory. This is a thing to live for." Man is to "thank and praise him now for everything" (*Sermons*, 240). But not only are inner states of praise called for; action and work are also: "It is not only prayer that gives God glory but work. Smiting on an anvil, sawing a beam, whitewashing a wall, driving horses, sweeping, scouring, everything gives God some glory if being in his grace you do it as your duty" (*Sermons*, 240).

The ultimacy of this single end can be seen especially from the vantage point of prospective death. From that standpoint lesser attachments are clearly lesser. If one loves these lesser things— stars, sunshine, home life, wife or husband, child, friend, money, fame, politics—"despair then: the world will do without you and you must do without the world, for you shall be where you cannot stir hand or foot to make it worse or better." And the ultimate question alone remains: "Do you love what is better than all these, to do God's work, to do good to others, to give alms, to make God's kingdom come? Make haste then, work while it is day, and despair of any other chance than this" (*Sermons*, 245). Death intensifies the single and ultimate end.

2.   *Inscape and Instress as Religious Concepts*

God is to be served, but first he must be found. He can disclose himself to anyone, of course, at any time or place through a special revelation or grace. But the creator who is to be served has made his discovery universally possible in a general revelation through the created world. He is immanent and omnipresent. Here the two notions of inscape and instress, so important for Hopkins's poetics, are relevant as religious concepts as well, for they suggest the modes in which divine presence can be sensed.

There is no need to dwell on elaborate definitions of these terms as has been much done already by others. I want to move quickly to their religious import.

Hopkins himself refers to inscape as simply "design, pattern,"[13] with the provision that it is always "individually-distinctive."[14] John Pick incorporates these two aspects of inscape when he says of Hopkins that "usually he employs the word to indicate the essential individuality and particularity or 'selfhood' of a thing working itself out and expressing itself in design and pattern."[15] Inscape, then, is a formal element. Instress, on the other hand, is a dynamic element, the tendency or power of a thing to manifest its unique being. A good glossary of Hopkinsian words describes instress as "the forceful impression made on a beholder by the inner energies of a thing's being."[16] Instress seems to suggest at once the enclosed inner power of a thing's unique being and the seething urge of this power to break into conscious impressions.

Thus simple definitions are quite possible. Gardner uses the following: for inscape, "unified pattern of essential attributes," and for instress, "energy or stress of being which holds the 'inscape' together."[17] With Professor Miller they could be reduced to "individual pattern" and "inner energy." Referring to Hopkins he says: "His celebrated terms 'inscape' and 'instress,' seems, when they apply to natural things at least, to refer, respectively, to the individual pattern of a thing and to the inner energy which upholds that pattern."[18] My suggestions, for brevity, would be "individually distinctive form" and "straining revelatory power."

Several points of clarifying gloss must be added. One is that inscape as form is to be understood not just as shape but as form in the metaphysical sense of a total interlacing of parts giving a thing its unity of organization. Second, the external sensory pattern of an inscape brings one into awareness of the inner nature of something. Thus Pick can say that "inscape" properly means "the essence or inner form of a thing as expressed in sensible pattern and design or outer form."[19] Thirdly, there is some controversy about whether inscape refers to the literally unique aspects of a thing, so that inscape is identical with Scotus's *haecceitas*, or whether it refers to the individually distinctive form of a species. Such a controversy seems misjoined because the two are not exclusive and are in fact both contained in the total form or inscape of a thing. Sometimes Hopkins stresses one, sometimes the other. In any case, the total form of a thing, say a bluebell, would have to include both the species's distinctiveness, that is, the "bluebellishness" of a bluebell; and the unique distinctiveness, that is, the particularity of a single bluebell which we might name Bluebell. Finally, there is a close connection between inscape and instress, for it is the instress of a thing which pommels its inner nature into our consciousness through the sensory pattern. "The inner pressure of instress, permeating nature, is the true source of inscape, and brought into the open by it."[20] Thus inscape and instress are polar terms. Instress without inscape is wild, but inscape without instress is frozen.

The transition to the religious significance of these concepts is in Hopkins's belief that God is the deviser of the inscapes in nature and the ultimate power behind the instresses in nature. What this belief suggests about God's nature I shall touch on later. Here I am interested in how they are related to man's finding of God. How, one may ask, is this vast realm of created being, with its myriads of inscapes and permeation of instresses, suited to man's discovery of God?

First, every inscape, as an individuality in a unified pattern, models for us the great individuality in unity which is God himself. God's maximal perfection is unique, and he also unifies maximal diversity in his conceptual understanding; and so each thing's inscape can serve as mirror or symbol of the divine being. "See God," Loyola enjoins, "living in His creatures: in matter, giving it existence, in plants, giving them life, in animals, giving them consciousness, in men, giving them intelligence." And as he is mirrored in these things, so he can be discovered in one's own being: "So He lives in me, giving me existence, life, consciousness, intelligence."[21]

Second, by virtue of inscape and instress, things can be said to have meaning and value, and so they can remind everyone of the goodness of God. All can see that they are in a value-laden universe, one in which facts and value intermesh. Without instress and inscape things would be meaningless—this seems to be Hopkins's point in his early college essay on Parmenides where he discusses instress. Hopkins writes: "His great text, which he repeats with religious conviction, is that Being is and Not-being is not—which perhaps one can say, a little over-defining his meaning, means that all things are upheld by instress and are meaningless without it. ... His feeling for instress... and for inscape/is most striking."[22] Whether Hopkins is right about Parmenides or not, his own view is that instress and inscape signify the convertibility of being and value, the universality of goodness in the creation.

But not only can these aspects of things mirror and remind, they can also initiate religious experience and so lead one to God in the first place. People are brought to God, Hopkins believes, "by God's particular will becoming known to them." Yet he asks in a sermon on 21 September 1879, "How does it become known?" and answers: "in a thousand ways, as many ways as there are men. Books, example, miracle etc" (*Sermons*, 25). Among these "thousand ways" is surely the experience of inscape and instress in created things.

Not only can these aspects of the world trigger religious experience in the first place, but they can set in motion a recurrence of reflection and experience carrying the seeker into continuing, deepening modes of experience. Hopkins views the creation as existing in a ladder of excellences culminating in the perfection of God himself. It is progression upward and outward into this scale of being that may be launched by the instress of inscapes into one's consciousness. In the following passage, Hopkins is speaking of inscapes in art, but one may take his words to refer to things generally: "It is only by bringing in the infinite that... a just judgment can be made...; and in this ordinary view of them... they have an absolute excellence in them and are steps in a scale of infinite and inexhaustible excellence."[23]

The created world, then, with its manifold inscapes and instresses that pervade it, is an inexhaustible resource for the discovery of God.

3. Providence and Evil

Now the darker side must be told. The foregoing, simple account of divine discovery is an account of an ideal situation. Universal awareness of God directly through creation is what would occur in the idyllic realm that Hopkins calls the original commonwealth or kingdom of God. Such natural awareness is very possible now; but a cloud of darkness has partially spread over the world, screening its otherwise brilliant light. For various reasons, God's presence is obscured, his providence clouded, his way inscrutable. These reasons must be cited, but first the way in which Hopkins speaks of this partial dimming of God's providence ought to be sampled. He likes the figures of light and dark, day and night. In one of his sermons he discourses vividly about the night that has fallen upon the world: "This life is night, it is night and not day; we are like sleepers in the nighttime, we are like men that walk in the dark. ... Life then is night, although he bids us walk in it as if it were day. ... This life is night, it is a night, it is a dark time. It is so because the truth of things is either dimly seen or not seen at all" (*Sermons*, 39).

In harsher words, Hopkins can speak of "this world of evil and mischance." He believes unfailingly in divine providence and has faith that it will be fulfilled ultimately. "In the meantime [, however,] God's providence is dark and we cannot hope to know the why and wherefore of all that is allowed to befall us" (*Sermons*, 92). We must live through this life of night with such limited light as is available to us.

There are several reasons for this nighttime of the world. The most obvious one is the fall of man into evil. "With that the contract with God was broken, the commonwealth undone, the kingdom divided and brought to desolation" (*Sermons*, 67). By his own evil acts man has spoiled the creation and separated himself from close union with God. He lives in shadows partly of his own making.

A second reason is the prevalence of what is called natural evil. The creation of finite things operating under regular causal laws brings with it imperfections and the possibility of natural catastrophes. To illustrate Hopkins's brooding sense of this aspect of nature, I must use a passage that is somewhat lengthier than the ones I have been utilizing; but the whole must be given to capture his graphic description of natural evil. Hopkins begins by reminding us once again to "search the whole world and you will find it a million-million fold contrivance of providence planned for our use and patterned for our admiration." To question this munificence is not the point. Yet immediately following this statement, the sermon continues:

> But yet this providence is imperfect, plainly imperfect. The sun shines too long and withers the harvest, the rain is too heavy and rots it or in floods spreading washes it away; the air and water carry in their currents the poison of disease; there are poison plants, venomous snakes and scorpions; the beasts our subjects rebel, not only the bloodthirsty tiger that slaughters yearly its thousands, but even the bull will gore and the stallion bite or strike; at night the moon sometimes has no light to give, at others the clouds darken her;.... [T]he coalpits and oilwells are full of explosions, fires, and outbreaks of sudden death, the sea of storms and wrecks, the snow has avalanches, the earth landslips; we contend with cold, want, weakness, hunger, disease, death, and often we fight a losing battle, never a triumphant one; everything is full of fault, flaw, imperfection, shortcoming; as many marks as there are of God's wisdom in providing for us so many marks there may be set against them of more being needed still, of something having made of this very providence a shattered frame and a broken web.
>
> (*Sermons*, 90)

Man's fall and natural evil, though permitted by God, can be viewed as coming outside his direct immanent purpose and activity. But Hopkins also sees God as mysteriously involved in certain ways in the darkness that enshrouds man. For one thing God often, for his own good reasons, holds aloof, keeps distant, does not reveal himself. He is *deus obscondita*. In biblical imagery, God is one who often hides himself: "Verily thou art a God that hidest thyself."[24] Such a circumstance compounds the difficulty, for even if one could overcome his sin and adjust to natural evil, he might still feel confused, empty, estranged, because of God's distance and silence. As it is, the night is only shaded the more.

This conception is complex enough; yet there is still a subtler mysterious way of God that is involved. Not only does he hide himself on occasion, but sometimes he chooses to disclose himself only through the very darkest elements of life—the violence and destruction in nature, the suffering and tragedy of human life. He is the God not just of the sun but of the storm. "As violence and destruction are part of God's purpose in the physical world, so also in his dealings with the body and soul of man He shows rude mastery... as well as tender mercy."[25] These words describe perhaps Hopkins's most distinctive emphasis in this entire topic. God can buffet and hound and add to the darkness. He can show hard ways in the accomplishment of his will.

Such then is the human condition: to live in a world where God's presence is potentially close, universal, and knowable, but in which, for human, natural, and divine reasons, God may be distant, difficult, and unknown. Providence is a shining glass, but we see through the glass darkly.

While this discussion is at this nadir dimension, one may ask whether there is in Hopkins anything like a theodicy, that is, a more or less formal explanation of evil in a world created by divine good. That Hopkins was concerned with evil is abundantly obvious. Gardner, in fact, says that the problem of evil is something with which "the mind of Hopkins was always deeply engaged."[26] But one can, of course, be deeply engaged with evil in relation to the practical religious life without being preoccupied with the purely logical aspects of theodicy. Nevertheless, there are some interesting hints in Hopkins which can be explored for the latter purpose. And while I, and Hopkins, would not claim originality here, the suggestions are worth setting out as part of Hopkins's working philosophy of religion.

First of all, there are several contentions, sometimes held, that could not be acceptable to Hopkins as a Christian realist. He could not, for instance, deny the reality of evil. Quite the opposite accentuation, in fact, stands out in his work. Nor can he, like Plato or any other believer in a finite uncreating God, hold that evil is some necessity, rigidity, or impairment inherent in the uncreated world's very structure, so that God too struggles with it as men do. Nor can Hopkins, with Manichaean dualism, hold that evil is equivalent with materiality; for spiritual beings both perform and experience evil, so that it is a reality in the spiritual realm as well as the physical. Counter to these views, a Christian theodicy like that of Hopkins must hold that God is the creator of all that is, that evil is real, and yet that God is not the immediate cause of evil.

That God is not the immediate cause of evil is unmistakably evident in "The Wreck of the Deutschland." Despite the evil of the shipwreck, as seen from a human viewpoint, Hopkins can still speak in stanza thirty-one of "a lovely-felicitous Providence", and then describe God in stanza thirty-three as endowed

> With a mercy that outrides
> The all of water, an ark
> For the listener; for the lingerer with a love glides
> Lower than death and the dark.

But what is needed to amplify this claim is a way of saying consistently, both that God is the creator of all and that he is not the direct cause of evil. Such a way is open to Hopkins by saying that God creates the conditions that make evil a possibility, but he does not himself employ those conditions to actualize the possible evil. The created conditions that make evil possible are twofold: man's affective nature, including his free will and his natural desire, and certain structural features in the objective order of nature.

The chief human condition making evil possible is man's free will. Hopkins certainly attributes much evil to man's own doing. In typical phrases, he says "we misshape his face and make God's image hideous," and "we are blotted, we are scribbled over with fowlness and blasphemy." And to anyone who would claim that this evil is itself a kind of necessity in us, he proclaims not so: for "what we have not done yet we can do now, what we have done badly hitherto we can do well henceforward, we can repent our sins and begin to give God glory" (*Sermons*, 240). This explanation by free will of course sums up the classic Christian defense on this problem, and Hopkins adheres to it.

There is another human trait involved in evil's occurrence, and that is what one might call man's over-desire and over-expectation. Man gets his heart set, as he ought not to, on various passing natural goods; and then when they do not materialize, he feels distress which he calls evil. But a more sensible desiring pattern would eliminate or prevent such evil. As Loyola says in the *Spiritual Exercises*, to which Hopkins adheres: "Therefore we need to train ouselves to be impartial in our attitude towards all created reality.... So that, as far as we are concerned, we do not set our heart on good health as against bad health, prosperity as against poverty, a good reputation as against a bad one, a long life as against a short one, and so on."[27] This point is relevant not only to the practical life of renunciation but to formal theodicy as well. Much evil is only seeming evil, which would not come to be in the first place if life were approached with proper restraint rather than egoistic demands.

Some Christians hold that free agency is the only explanation of evil needed. Natural evil, as distinguished from moral evil, is assigned to the activity of other fallen spiritual beings, namely, Satan and his cohorts. Hopkins's beliefs would permit this, since his belief about angels seems fully orthodox. Besides this possibility, however, there is another common point in Christian theodicy, namely, that natural conditions themselves cause some evil. The reasoning is this: Man's spiritual life requires an orderly, lawful realm of nature in which to function and grow; but this lawful order sometimes constricts human purpose, and thus evil is permitted but not directly caused by God. Hopkins's acceptance of this point is implicit but clear in "The Wreck of the Deutschland." An example, from stanza seventeen, is this:

> They fought against God's cold—
> And they could not and fell to the deck
> (Crushed them) or water (and drowned them) or rolled
> With the sea-romp over the wreck.

God creates and controls nature, but its lawful orderliness allows evil. Yet God is above all of nature's ways despite their occasional inexplicable severity, stanza twenty-one:

> Surf, snow, river and earth
> Gnashed: but thou art above, thou Orion of light.

This leads to a further step required in the whole argument. Since God created free agents and the realm of nature, he might be charged with being, if not the proximate, at least the remote cause of evil. Therefore, it must be held that God had a reason, rooted in good, for thus creating. The reason is that there is a greater potential for the realization of good with the possibility of evil than without it. In the case of human good, one can hold that it is far better to be a free agent than an automaton and far better to grow through problems and perils than to be isolated from them. But one is not committed to saying that human good is the only good to be considered in this criterion. God may be believed to have his own good ends that vindicate the possibility of evil. And at this point reason passes into faith, for a Christian believes that God has purposes for good which are beyond our fathoming.

But of the human good in particular, one affirmation resounds in Hopkins, namely, that the highest good is possible despite great evil. And if such a good requires such a possibility, then that is sufficient vindication. What is that good? It can include moral virtue, and there is much in Hopkins on moral strength acquired through storm. But above all, it is the realization of God. This realization is the good that evil can yield—indeed the highest good. Of the tall nun on the Deutschland, Hopkins says, with simple adequacy: "Well, she has thee for the pain." This line says everything. But an expansion of it from a sermon is worth quoting in conclusion, a conclusion that typically highlights both truth and practicality on this topic. Why is there evil, one asks?

> Let us not now enquire, brethren, why this should be; we most sadly feel and know that so it is. But there is good in it; for if we were not forced from time to time to feel our need of God and our dependence on him, we should most of us cease to pray to him and to thank him. If he did everything we should treat him as though he did nothing, whereas now that he does not do all we are brought to remember how much he does.
>
> (*Sermons*, 90-91)

4. Life as Sacrifice

In view of the precariousness of nature and human aspiration, and the evil to which we are prone, Hopkins came to see the key to the spiritual life to be sacrifice—sacrifice of what one would otherwise be attached to by natural desire, sacrifice for the kingdom of God. Thus in his own life he could partially reconcile himself to the lack of poetic activity and fame; a higher service was being carried out. The deeply paradoxical but genuine spiritual truth is that sacrifice, though painful and even bitter, could nevertheless result in a real, even unexpected, attainment at a different level.

Christ is for Hopkins the model of sacrifice, however else he might be interpreted theologically. Christ succeeded by being humanly unsuccessful. Christ's sacrifice of his own bliss, his emptying of himself for others, is the example to be followed. In Hopkins's words:

> He emptied or exhausted himself so far as that was possible, of Godhead and behaved only as God's slave, as his creature, as man, which also he was, and then being in the guise of man humbled himself to death, the death of the cross. It is this holding of himself back, and not snatching at the truest and highest good, the good that was his right,... which seems to me the root of all his holiness and the imitation of this the root of all moral good in other men.[28]

And so Christ lived among men not as a proud master but as a humble servant. "Poor was his station, laborious his life, bitter his ending: through poverty, through labour, through crucifixion his majesty of nature more shines" (Sermons, 37).

For the life of the religious aspirant who would follow Christ's example, this idea of the rewards of sacrifice would mean a greater willingness to sacrifice coveted earthly goods. "In meditating on the Crucifixion," Hopkins says, "I saw how my asking to be raised to a higher degree of grace was asking also to be lifted on a higher cross" (Sermons, 254). It means also a readiness to bear the burdens of suffering, of hardship, of disappointment, of charity. For "those who find themselves born to the blessings and avail themselves of those blessings know they must be born to bear the burdens and that it is their duty to bear them" (Sermons, 56). It means as well that at all times one's desires, passions, and egoism must be kept in proper check under the control of one's higher spiritual nature. As the Spiritual Exercises puts it, one is "to overcome oneself, that is, to subject the sensual nature to reason, and in general to ensure that all our lower appetites are under the control of our higher powers."[29]

Life as sacrifice does not exhaust all there is to say about religious living. But it is a central theme in the practical side of Hopkins's philosophy of religion.

5. *Preincarnation and Divine Attributes*

Christ is interpreted by Hopkins not only as a model of sacrifice for human beings to follow but as central to a far wider cosmic event. In this regard Hopkins is led to some unusual Christological speculations. The most common Christian view in tradition is that Christ was incarnated in human form to redeem fallen man. But for Hopkins Christ has other cosmic roles as well.

The first point is that Christ is the first object of created being, created to glorify God. That is, Christ does not remain an unchanging internal part of the Trinity but is projected in an objective created nature to reflect God and model the subsequent creation. In one of his essays Hopkins puts it this way: "Man himself was created for Christ as Christ's created nature for God. And in this way Christ is the firstborn among creatures. ... The first intention then of God outside himself or, as they say, *ad extra*, outwards, the first outstress of God's power, was Christ" (*Sermons*, 196-97). Christ is thus the first of created natures; and his essence is present throughout the rest of creation, unifying it and mirroring it back to God. This created nature of Christ Hopkins saw as a universal incarnational presence. As Christopher Devlin points out, "He saw creation as dependent upon the decree of the incarnation, and not the other way round. The worlds of angels and of men were created as fields for Christ in which to exercise his adoration of the Father" (*Sermons*, 109).

This view of Christ means, furthermore, that Christ was present in creation, was incarnated before the period of the current cosmos and man. He was preincarnated, if one may speak thus, in an earlier age, since there certainly was such an age in Hopkins's belief. This preincarnation, as Devlin understands it, was apparently in a material form as well (see *Sermons*, 112). In this preincarnation Christ had the function of glorifying God through unfallen beings and of redeeming fallen ones like Lucifer.

This notion of preincarnation leads Devlin to a further speculative observation in a contemporary vogue, a speculation that presumably involves the idea of plural incarnation. He writes, by way of a reticent afterthought:

> Space-travel and the discovery of other planets are now possibilities that have to be taken into account. In the event (however unlikely) of some form of rational life being found on another planet, the question of the redemption would be bound to arise. If Hopkins's distinction were valid, one would not have to suppose that the creatures of another planet had been deprived of the light of the Incarnation because they had had no historical knowledge of Christ's life and death on earth.
>
> (*Sermons*, 115)

Finally, this view of Christ means for Hopkins that incarnation has the function of drawing men to God independently of whether man fell into sin or not. "His [Hopkins's] mind leaped to the conclusion that redemption or sacrifice of some sort, so as to give an opportunity for love by free choice, would have been necessary even had there been no sin" (*Sermons*, 110). In fact man has fallen into sin, so Christ is redeemer in the traditional sense. But he would have, and has, a restoring role beyond this one.

Hopkins was influenced and aided in this interpretation by the young French mystic, Maria Lataste, who had died at the age of twenty-five only three years after Hopkins's birth. Maria spoke of two movements of creation, one toward man and the other toward God. It would be helpful to look at a passage of hers on this point. I give it in French, with a translation in a footnote.

> L'homme vient de Dieu et doit retourner à Dieu. Il y a deux mouvements en l'homme: de son être créé par Dieu vers l'existence et de son être existant vers Dieu. Ces deux mouvements sont donnés à l'homme par Dieu; et par ces deux mouvements, l'homme, s'il le veut, retournera infailliblement à Dieu. Je dis s'il le veut, parce que l'homme peut changer la direction de ce mouvement.[30]

In the first movement man receives being and lives within a given framework. But the second movement, that of returning to God, is open to choice by virtue of man's liberty. Living as he now does under earthly conditions with earthly interests, man might not return in spirit, and this failure to return may occur even in the absence of a datable fall or overt rebellion. Hopkins came to think therefore that Christ's love and sacrifice were necessary to show man the way back and to facilitate his return, so that man would know fully the genuine options for his free will. The fact that man has fallen has added further complications to the return. But the second movement would be, and is, necessary in any case.

Hopkins wrote a Welsh poem that celebrates the return to God. It clearly shows that the return is a "praise-return" and not only a gratitude for recovery from sin.

> Not because Thou hast redeemed me do I love Thee, Lord,
> . . . .
> Infinite grief has Thou endured, and pain and sweat on my behalf,
> Sinner that I am—even unto death for my sake.
> . . . .
> But just as Thou didst love me, so shall I love Thee and *do*
>   love Thee,
> Only because Thou art God and art to me a Ruler.[31]

The concept of preincarnation amplifies, I think, the Christocentric character of Hopkins's philosophy of religion.

Some aspects of God's nature, according to Hopkins, have been implicit in what has been said so far, for example, that God is sovereign and benevolent, that he is immanent and omnipresent in the various inscapes and instresses of creation, that he sometimes hides his clear image from man, that he makes conditions for possible evil but is not the direct cause of evil, that he ordains objective incarnation and hence creation to mirror his goodness. Some other points, however, are also prominent in Hopkins's thinking.

Hopkins holds to what has been called the classical or orthodox conception of God. One doctrine in this view is that God creates the world out of nothing, *ex nihilo* (see *Sermons*, 238). This means, among other things, that there is absolutely no rival to God in priority of being, for all else in creation is his self-initiated production.

God is also eternal in this view, that is, out of time altogether, not living in or through time. There is no temporal aspect in God, as a Whiteheadian would have it, though God knows time in his essence. "Le passé, le présent et l'avenir ne sont pour Dieu qu'une seule et même chose; pour lui, l'avenir et le passé sont toujours présents."[32] This means that creation, which might appear to us to be a temporal process, or at least to have a temporal dimension, occurs for God all at once, as it were, and eternally. Hopkins puts it this way: "There is no relation between any duration of time and the duration of God. ...God from every point, so to say, of his being creates all things" (Sermons, 196). Also God's knowledge, by which he knows all things, is not acquired as new events happen in time but is a single and eternal act in his mind. An early unfinished poem entitled "Shakspere" speaks of "God... whose dateless thought must chart/All time at once and span the distant goals" (Poems, no. 126).

Another aspect of the classical idea of God is that God is absolutely self-sufficient in his being, with no relations to the world which add anything to his perfection. He is in no need of our being or service. Man honors God even though "the honour is like none, less than a buttercup to a king; the service is of no service to him. In other words he does not need it. He has infinite glory without it and what is infinite can be made no bigger" (Sermons, 239). God, because of his infinite goodness and majesty, is to be served by man for that reason and not because such service makes a contribution to God.

Providence, in the sense of wise superintendence and provision, is of course a traditional attribute. One interesting feature of Hopkins's view of this attribute is that he can speak of God's having a duty of providence. Hopkins pictures the original creation as a kind of commonwealth with everyone participating. God too is a participant, albeit as head. This portrayal suggests that God, although sovereign and self-sufficient, enters into an immanent participant's role in the commonwealth. All have duties in the commonwealth, and so Hopkins, unlike Kant, thinks of God as having duty, albeit self-chosen.

> A commonwealth, we said, was bound together by duty; the sovereign was bound by duty as the subject. Here then what was the duty God undertook?—Providence. That was the part, function, office, and duty in that commonwealth God took upon himself,

> first to foresee both his and man's joint and common good, then by
> his policy and legislation to bring it to pass.
>
> (*Sermons*, 59)

Thus God and man, though not ontologically interdependent, are joint obligatees in the commonwealth of creation.

Foreknowledge and predestination are further attributes of God which Hopkins affirms. God foresees from all eternity what will happen in what man calls the future. And God settles the outcomes of our lives on the basis of our choices. Neither of these doctrines is intended to mean determinism in the sense of negating free will. But more on this vexing problem must await the next section.

Finally, I should like to mention a point in the words of Professor Miller. It is the individuality of perfection that characterizes God in a superlative way.

> God's infinity and his "selfexistence" consists not so much in his possession of some universal quality like "being," "power," or "will" (though he has these too), as in his possession of the most highly patterned self of all. His pattern is infinitely complex, and therefore he contains in himself the matrices for all possible and actual creatures, including man. God vibrates simultaneously at all possible pitches.[33]

Whitehead holds that a coherent metaphysical scheme must show that all entities, including God, illustrate common metaphysical principles without making God, as is often done, an unwarranted exception. On many points Hopkins's view of God is poles apart from that of Whitehead. But on this metaphysical requirement, if it is a requirement, there is perhaps a similarity. For to Hopkins, God illustrates individuality of perfection just as every other being does. The only difference is that God is the superlative case.

These various attributes mentioned here do not compose a total doctrine of God. For example, there would have to be added traditional Catholic teachings about God which Hopkins took for granted. But these aspects do indicate some concerns that were central to him.

6. Self and Freedom

From the concept of God, the study turns to the self that is engaged in religious movement. There appear to be, in Hopkins's thinking, three more or less unified components of human selfhood. I shall introduce these through a relevant quotation from his essay, "On Personality, Grace, and Free Will":

> Self is the intrinsic oneness of a thing, which is prior to its being and does not result from it *ipso facto*, does not result, I mean, from its having independent being.... Now a bare self, to which no nature has yet been added, which is not yet clothed or overlaid with a nature, is indeed nothing, a zero, in the score of account of existence, but as possible it is positive, like a positive infinitesimal, and intrinsically different from every other self. For in the world, besides natures or essences or 'inscapes' and the selves... which wear and 'fetch' or instance them, there is still something else—fact or fate.
>
> (*Sermons*, 146)

The first and basic component in a person is the ideal self envisioned in the mind of God. This possible self is the one God desires one to be, and it is always the goal that one most deeply aspires to be. Man seeks to be "in God's eye what in God's eye he is." This goal is the "immortal diamond" man is to recover in its pure luster. But this possibility has no existential reality by itself. It serves rather as the model for a created being designed to reflect or duplicate it fully. The actually created being is endowed with a human nature; the bare self is "clothed" with a human essence—which is the second component. The third component is the individual facticity of each self's career in the temporal order. This individual facticity does not, due to choice and other influences, reflect very fully the original self.

Central to the full existential reality of human selfhood, with its ideal model, its human nature, and its unique facticity, is freedom of will. By this freedom, man can shape his career, can journey toward or away from his ideal self. Selves, as Hopkins conceives of them, "cannot appear except in a rational, to speak more to the point/

in a free/nature" (*Sermons*, 147). With this freedom man is in a
dynamic state, a process: he is moving either farther from or closer
to the union with his ideal model in God. "Personality" is his term
for this dynamic selfhood; personality is the self, with its human
nature and its freedom, choosing its course in the movements of
creation. "Personality, then," as Devlin interprets it, "is movement
from the ideal to the actual, and back from the actual to the ideal
.... Personality is thus a journey into ever-increasing never-ending
self-realization" (*Sermons*, 350).

Concerning Hopkins's view of freedom, there are three special
problems on which I should like to comment. The first is the relation
of freedom and necessity. This relationship is something that evi-
dently concerned Hopkins considerably, for he discusses it in a
letter to Bridges and offers the following resolution: "Hereby, I
may tell you, hangs a very profound question treated by Duns
Scotus, who shews that freedom is compatible with necessity. And
besides, common sense tells you that though if you say A_1 you
cannot help saying A_2 yet you can help saying $A_1 + A_2$ at all; you
could have said $B_1 + B_2$ or $C_1 + C_2$ etc."[34] Hopkins apparently has
in mind here logical necessity. The symbols would have to be in-
stanced, of course, in order to be genuine examples of logical necessity, but logical necessity is apparently what he means. It is not
reasonable to think he means that causal necessity can be made
compatible with freedom, for such necessity would be the opposite
of free will as he conceives of it. He does not appear to be a soft
determinist. Still it is interesting to note that he does hold logical
necessity to be quite consistent with free will. He would not be
moved by a rationalist seeking to eliminate free will through logical
necessity, or by an empiricist abandoning logical necessity because
of freedom.

The second problem is that of reconciling the causal efficacy of
divine grace with genuine free will. That is, as Devlin frames the
question: "How can God move a man's free will to attain a destiny
beyond the power of his nature, and yet leave it free and responsible
for its actions?" (*Sermons*, 338). The answer Hopkins upholds,
following Scotus, is to distinguish two aspects of the will, namely,
affective will and elective will (see Devlin's observations in *Sermons*,
339). By the affective will one is predisposed to crave God and be
open to his influence. The elective will is the capacity for genuine

free choice. God's causation of grace operates on man but is held then in abeyance to provide a genuine opportunity for man to accept or reject. One philosophical consequence of this view is that there is not in Hopkins a sharp opposition between will and inclination, as there might be in a Kantian. One's deepest inclination is desire for God, and moral duty is to follow this inclination rather than turn away from it. Such a view of will, Devlin explains, is far more in keeping with Catholic spirituality than is the image of a completely autonomous "lonely will struggling grimly against all that is most attractive to his higher nature" (*Sermons*, 118).

The third problem is that of man's freedom and God's foreknowledge. The problem is whether total foreknowledge disallows genuine alternatives for free will. Hopkins certainly wants to hold to God's omniscience. He would agree with Maria Lataste: "Il est certain que Dieu sait tout de tout éternité, et qu'il connaît part conséquent quels sont ceux qui seront rebelles."[35] Nevertheless, to accept free will fully one must also believe:

> Or, cette prévision de Dieu n'influe en rien sur la réprobation des hommes, car elle n'a aucune action sur l'homme qui conserve tout sa liberté, et peut abuser ou non des grâces de Dieu. ... C'est parce que l'homme se perd que Dieu le prévoit, et non parce que Dieu le prévoit que l'homme se perd et se damne. Dieu donne des grâces, mais il laisse avec elles la liberté, et l'homme, en donnant ou refusant sa correspondance a ces grâces, se damne ou se sauve librement.[36]

But how can there be exact foreknowledge without exact determination of how man will decide? Devlin suggests the Scotist solution as being Hopkins's view, namely, that "man's free decisions are taken out of time, and that in them God's will and man's will concur simultaneously, God's previous knowledge of these decisions being— as the Scotists say—'flexible' to either alternative: 'God not only knows what may or may not happen, but he knows it *in such a way that* it may or may not happen'" (*Sermons*, 307). It is not clear from this passage whether God's previous knowledge includes knowledge of exactly which of the alternatives that may or may not happen man will in fact choose. The last part of the quotation suggests that it might not; but the first part suggests that it might, especially in the light of the peculiar view that "man's free decisions are taken out of time." The classical doctrine is that God's knowledge does include all such knowledge and that this knowledge is in no way inconsistent with freedom: foreknowing a decision simply does not compel that decision to happen. I suspect Hopkins intended to hold the classical doctrine and to avow no inconsistency. On the other hand, if one of the two ideas, foreknowledge and freedom, would have to be redefined, it might be that for him the precise character of foreknowledge would be the one more open to further analysis. It is doubtful that he would want to alter the ringing affirmation of freedom given by St. Ignatius Loyola: "Nor should we talk so much about grace and with such insistence on it as to give rise to the poisonous view that destroys freedom. ... But our language and way of speaking should not be such that the value of our activities and the reality of human freedom might be in any way impaired or disregarded."[37] The same tone is sounded in Hopkins's own poetic lines, though they cannot be taken as finished analytical philosophy:

> Man lives that list, that leaning in the will
> No wisdom can forecast by gauge or guess,
> The selfless self of self, most strange, most still,
> Fast furled and all foredrawn to No or Yes.
> ("On the Portrait of Two Beautiful Young People")

7.　*Philosophical Realism*

The pervasive, overarching perspective behind Hopkins's philosophical thought is that of realism, metaphysical and epistemological. He defends realism in an early essay, "The Probable Future of Metaphysics,"[38] and this persuasion is deepened and clarified by the studies he undertook later. Much later, to Bridges, he can identify himself under the rubric, "we Aristotelian Catholics,"[39] clearly a realist tradition.

Professor Todd K. Bender interprets the essay mentioned as supporting a kind of phenomenalism, almost a Berkeleyan type. For example, he writes:

Hopkins' undergraduate essay, "The Probable Future of Metaphysics," ...shows how thoroughly he had accepted the idea that sensory impressions are not necessarily an accurate report of the objective world.... In short, Hopkins assumes that our mental activity is distinct from the material world.... We have no way of knowing what is "really" outside the mind.[40]

But I think Professor Bender seriously misinterprets the principal import of this essay. For one thing, it was written the year after Hopkins's conversion to Catholicism when he may be presumed to have intended a break away from the prevailing Oxford mentalism and movement toward Catholic realism, even though his understanding of this tradition was not yet systematically developed. Far more important, however, the import of the essay is not to defend phenomenalism but to defend metaphysics by opposing three schools of thought which seek to undermine it, namely, postivism, Kantianism, and certain kinds of idealism. Hopkins identifies himself with realism in this effort. He even uses the term "the new realism," a term that came to be so prominent in early twentieth-century philosophy. As it turned out, Hopkins was not very accurate in forecasting the issues that would preoccupy the new realism when it emerged at the turn of the century in the hands of Moore, Russell, and others. But he strongly affirms realism and the legitimacy of metaphysics which it upholds. The sorts of passages to which Professor Bender refers are intended mainly to discredit a materialistic explanation of mind, or "identity materialism" as it would be called today, rather than to support phenomenalism. This conception fits in well with realism, for realism opposes materialism as well as phenomenalism. The essay is unquestionably more Platonic than is characteristic of "Aristotelian Catholics," but this bias is understandable at the Oxford stage of Hopkins' life and does not in any case alter its realist tendency.

There are four great planks in traditional realism which are accepted by Hopkins. These are perceptual, formal, aesthetic, and religious. Perceptually, the objects of one's perception are objectively real, constituting an order of things not dependent on the mind. The world is a realm of existing, created beings, and our minds are oriented toward that objective order. Formally, the universals or forms of things are also aspects of this objective order and are not merely concepts or names in our minds. Although Hopkins stresses individuality in things, he does not reject forms or universals; individuality includes the individuality *of form*, the form *in* things. Aesthetically, not only is it the case that with beauty "these things were here and but the beholder wanting" ("Hurrahing in Harvest"), but the very subject of art is objective reality and not the artist's fancies. This point is an important one in Hopkins's aesthetics, for he says that "a kind of touchstone of the highest or most living art is seriousness; not gravity but the being in earnest with your subject—reality."[41] Religiously and climactically, God is objectively real, with his own eternal existence, and not a creation of our minds. These planks of realism became basic in Hopkins's mature philosophy.

As a part of this realism, and as a conclusion to this philosophical sketch, I should like to give a sample piece of philosophical analysis Hopkins left, one of the few he recorded though he was obviously a capable philosopher. This example is a kind of theistic argument which has some novel features. It is not worked out in precise logical form, probably because it occurs in retreat notes that have a different function. The function is not that of convincing a skeptical unbeliever but that of showing how a believer can trace out his faith rationally to God. With Anselm, it is a case of faith seeking understanding. It is a meditation on the "First Principle and Foundation" of the *Spiritual Exercises* (*Sermons*, 122-30), but I shall try to formulate the argumentational heart of it.

I would call it a cosmological argument, but this may be a misnomer. Hopkins says there are two rational avenues to God, one the consideration of outward nature, the other the consideration of inward selfhood. The former is most common (like Aquinas's five ways, presumably), but Hopkins is more impressed by the latter. So already a difference is revealed. The main feature of the inner self which impresses him is its individuality. The problem is how this individuality is to be accounted for. Thus the argument might be dubbed an argument from radical uniqueness of self.

There are, I believe, at least two axioms for the argument which Hopkins never states. One would be the principle of sufficient reason, namely, that there must be an adequate explanation of a thing's existing. An adequate explanation here means that there must be a cause with sufficient power and capacity to produce the thing in question. The other principle one might call the principle of sufficient likeness. Hopkins assumes that in order to produce something, a cause must be like the thing in question in relevant respects; otherwise it would not have the properties to produce that particular thing even if it had the power. In general, then, the argument holds that nowhere, except in God, is there sufficient power and sufficient likeness to produce the radically unique self.

The argument could move either from human nature as such or from my individually distinctive self. The argument from human nature runs thus:

> For human nature, being more highly pitched, selved, and distinctive than anything in the world, can have been developed, evolved, condensed, from the vastness of the world not anyhow or by the working of common powers but only by one of finer or higher pitch and determination than itself and certainly than any that elsewhere we see, for this power had to force forward the starting or stubborn elements to the one pitch required.
>
> (*Sermons*, 122-23)

But the phase of the argument which is dearest to Hopkins's mind is that of the individual self, that is, "my selfbeing, my consciousness and feeling of myself, that taste of myself, of *I* and *me*." Each of us is unique, "more distinctive than the taste of ale or alum, more distinctive than the smell of walnutleaf or camphor" (*Sermons*, 123).

Now the question is how to explain the existence of this radically unique self. Three possibilities appear: chance, self-existence, or external agency. "From what then do I with all my being and above all that taste of self, that selfbeing, come? Am I due (1) to chance? (2) to myself, as selfexistent? (3) to some extrinsic power?" (*Sermons*, 123). Hopkins argues against the first two options and then presumes that the extrinsic power must be God, presumably on the ground that nothing else meets the axioms stated above.

By "chance" Hopkins seems to mean the opposite of causal determination. Something happens by chance if it occurs without any definite causal influence. But chance, in this sense, he thinks, applies only to possibilities, which simply *are*, without being produced. Actual things with actual properties must be caused to be what they are in the existing world. This is an a priori consideration. But experience too confirms that things do not come into being without causes.

Nor is it plausible to think of oneself as self-existent. One occupies rather definite boundaries in space and time, as do all other beings in the order of nature. They are finite. But for a finite thing to produce itself or determine its own being, it would have to be operative before it existed, which conclusion is absurd. It cannot function until it is actualized, but this actualization requires another agent.

At this point Hopkins does not argue further that this extrinsic power must be God. A modern naturalistic critic would insist that, even if the previous reasoning were acceptable, the extrinsic power could simply be the realm of nature which is self-existent even though the finite items in it are not. Hopkins apparently intends the usual cosmological claim that the realm of nature is nothing other than these finite things, which are not self-existent; so that in finite things, either individually or collectively, there is no explanation of nature's very existence and therefore of any individual's existence. Furthermore, Hopkins has dwelt on the unique difference of his own being from every other thing in nature, so that even if nature had the power to account for his existence, it would not have the likeness. It would have to be shown, of course, that self or personality really is distinct from physical nature and cannot be reduced to bodily behavior. Hopkins does affirm this distinctness of self. But God is also personality, the great self that illustrates superlatively the unique perfection of selfhood. So God alone has sufficient power *and* likeness to account for finite selves.

There is still a further contention that can be related to the idea of radical uniqueness. In discussing the option of self-existence, Hopkins considers whether a person might not be self-existent on the ground of being part of a universal mind that *is* self-existent, as the Hegelians hold. He rejects this notion because such a mind, being universal, cannot be *"me"* in the fully distinctive sense. In language characteristic of existentialist criticisms of Hegel, he says: "The universal cannot taste this taste of self as I taste it" (*Sermons*, 125). But there is another criticism more pertinent to this formulation of the whole argument. Hopkins says that a universal mind would have to encompass all possible worlds as well as the actual world into its being. But then there would be no real existing difference between possible worlds and the actual world, which conclusion is absurd since it is plain a real difference does exist. Now the point is this: the whole actual world may be seen as a radically unique instance of being, differing from all other, merely possible, worlds. It too must therefore, like the unique self, have a sufficient cosmological explanation. In this case only a power capable of actualizing possible worlds, and with sufficient likeness to encompass these possibilities, can be the explanation. This description too fits the concept of God.

In summary, human nature is radically unique among existing natures; the individual self is radically unique among all beings; and the actual world is radically unique among possible worlds. All of these instances must be accounted for by an external agent that has both sufficient power of production and sufficient likeness of properties to produce those particular realities. Nothing natural or finite suffices. God, whose nature includes by concept creative power, unique selfhood, and the envisioning of all possibilities, stands as the sole explanation. Therefore, if these things exist, as they do, then God must exist.

In bringing this entire chapter to a close, I should like to quote a sentence from Barbara Hardy's first annual lecture before the Hopkins Society. The statement is made mainly in reference to the poems, but it is appropriate in terms of Hopkins's general thought as well. She says: "I believe passion in Hopkins is highly individual, while the facts, beliefs and modes of argument come from a common stock."[42] Hopkins's philosophy of religion is not perhaps original in the sense of being unprecedented, for it comes from a common stock. Still his tone is often interesting and sometimes intriguingly personal.

Epilogue

The inquiries in the previous chapters have been based on the thesis that the uniqueness and the greatness of Hopkins's religious poetry consists in its illumination of the human experience of encagement, naturation, and grace. Some elaboration of the thesis itself seems in order before closing.

It might be considered extravagant if one were to extend the appraisal just mentioned by saying that it applies, plainly and simply, to Hopkins *as a poet*; one would then have to bring in other perspectives, for example, poetic technique and diction, a view of the poems as literary works, historical comparisons, and so on. The extended thesis would not seem to me indefensible; but the range of the present study is limited to Hopkins's religious poetry, or, more accurately, to his poetry religiously viewed. And the interpretation of his uniqueness and greatness seems plausible on this plane at least.

This estimate would be strikingly supported, one would suppose, if it could be shown that Hopkins's poetry is, in the respect indicated, widely descriptive of human experience; or, to phrase the idea in the popular idiom, that the poetry demonstrates contemporary relevance, for example, by rendering a diagnosis of a common psychic ill and by testifying to the reality of a cure. Certainly relevance is no requirement for poetic greatness. We do not expect our poets to engage in universal generalizations, diagnoses, and prescriptions to merit the tribute of greatness. Their task is to be honest to whatever material they have, to present in dazzling imagery and sure technique the statement of their experiences. Thus, even if Hopkins were portraying only his own personal experience of which others were not cognizant, his handling of it as he did should be sufficient for poetic acclaim. Yet we do also ask whether a poet has struck the wider soundingboard of human experience; and we are inclined to think that if he has done so, his stature is increased, provided he has not done so at the expense of poetic skill.

It would be too much to suggest that a religious poet describes the *de facto* experience of all people. Religious experience is limited and diverse. In the nature of the case, the experience Hopkins depicts is a potentiality only—when we speak of mankind as a whole. Moreover, to say it is even a potentiality is a kind of normative judgment since it must presuppose a certain theological view of the world. Once these strictures have been acknowledged, however, it is possible to ask how universal this potentiality's intimation of this particular experience is for mankind. And it seems plausible to assume that the recognition of the potentiality is far wider than the *de facto* experience itself. This recognition may account for some of Hopkins's appeal despite the spiritual distance felt by many admirers.

But many things are potentialities only. So one cannot avoid the question, when thinking of contemporary relevance, of how much of mankind's *actual* experience is being described. A fully factual answer to this question would perhaps be a matter of religious sociology. Meanwhile, someone may proffer the opinion that there are many personal testimonies—written and unwritten, past and present, sophisticated and simple—which disclose that people share many aspects of Hopkins's experience or at least know what he is writing about. If such testimony does exist, it would constitute ample support for the appraisal I have proposed.

It is also possible to take the particular aspects of the total experience and relate these individually to contemporary culture. Most obvious for this kind of analysis is the encagement theme. Thus W. H. Gardner can claim unequivocally: "The truth is (though few are aware of it and not many will care to acknowledge it) that these astringent later sonnets crystallize that sense of frustration, of separation from God, which is the peculiar psychic disease of the twentieth century."[1] Not all analyses of this sort use religious terminology; but the secular counterparts sound similar motifs to those of Hopkins at this stage of the experience. One hears voluminous accounts of modern man's alienation, of his anomie, of his ennui, of his forlornness, of his anxiety, of his feeling of absurdity, of his hopelessness, of his search for meaning. Hopkins is akin to Kierkegaard in this prescience, though his output is too meager and too poetic to permit ranking him as a psychological cultural analyst per se.

Secular statements about the second phase, the self-effort or naturation phase, are even more abundant, possibly because their authors have abandoned any other source of solution. Countless are the urgings to work harder, to get going, to solve our own problems, to save ourselves. Hopkins's perspective is more sober: he knows that man always retains a well of creative power because man is the creature of ultimate creative power, but he also knows that this power is proportionately limited. Secular thought remains ambiguous about whether man has any power at all or whether his power is without bounds.

There is a very striking, if indirect, parallel to these first two Hopkinsian phases in a statement by John Rawls in his *A Theory of Justice*. The statement speaks first of a human plight, which statement is actually more akin to Hopkins than are many diagnoses, since Hopkins refers, in his encagement passages, not just to his time or our time but to the human condition as such. Then the statement highlights self-respect as a prerequisite for being able to cope with this human plight and to carry out one's duties and interests. Rawls writes:

> When we feel that our plans are of little value, we cannot pursue them with pleasure or take delight in their execution. Nor plagued by failure and self-doubt can we continue in our endeavors. It is clear then why self-respect is a primary good. Without it nothing may seem worth doing, or if some things have value for us, we lack the will to strive for them. All desire and activity becomes empty and vain, and we sink into apathy and cynicism. Therefore the parties in the original position would wish to avoid at almost any cost the social conditions that undermine self-respect.[2]

As for the third phase, testimonies to grace are virtually equivalent to most religion itself. So evidence from that quarter is obvious. What is less obvious is the secular counterpart of this phase. Yet such testimonials are also frequent. The typical model here might run: "It is not I alone who deserves the credit, but the parents who reared me, the teachers who taught me, the country which gave me opportunities, the gifts which nature bestowed on me, etc." Paeans to grace abound even where God is purged.

The point in referring to these religious and secular echoings of Hopkins's themes is simply to suggest that he presages what many others have also come to say when confronting the human condition, current or perennial, and hence to underscore Hopkins's relevance.

It is in this framework of the ENG experience that I believe certain other notable estimates of Hopkins's uniqueness and greatness should be subsumed. For example, Professor Downes gives the following appraisal of Hopkins's achievement: "Finally, I should like to suggest that of all those aspects of Hopkins one might examine, and the list is a long and imposing one (esthetics, psychology, poetic theory and practice, theology and personality), the central and unifying notion is the human apprehension of the divine subsidy upholding and continuing created nature."[3] In the framework of this study, the divine upholding of nature is an assumed theological undergirding in all phases of the ENG experience and a more conscious apprehension in some of its moments. But this theological undergirding is not the whole of the experience that Hopkins conveys to us. Human terror and struggle and grace-experience would be meaningless without divine subsidy of nature; but we apprehend the divine subsidy through them.

Likewise can one view Hopkins's sensitivity to beauty in nature. Some find Hopkins's greatness as a religious poet to consist in his extraordinary alertness to the individualities and sensuous designs in natural things, especially his seeing of these as mirroring the divine image. There is much to be said for this sensitivity as an independent reason for greatness if one were focusing, for example, on Hopkins's early journal, which is almost exclusively devoted to sensuous description of natural things, or on his early nature sonnets taken in isolation. But when one focuses on the later poems as well as the earlier and sees the nature poems as integral to the larger corpus, he will see Hopkins's sensuous delight in nature as one element among others in the second and third phases of the ENG experience. Thus Gardner compares Hopkins in this regard not to nature poets but to St. Francis: "The Franciscans stressed the nearness of God, the pervading spirit of love, and like St. Francis himself they cordially greeted the 'image' or 'vestige' of God in all created things, animate and inanimate. In this respect, Hopkins resembled St. Francis."[4]

Analogous remarks would be appropriate concerning the Christo-centric aspect of Hopkins's religious poetry, which aspect others have found to constitute its central meaning. Other possibilities might also come to mind for interpreting its central meaning. There is no need to review them all. The point in mentioning these alter-native conceptions is not to oppose them but only to suggest that this framework of interpretation can accommodate them.

The ENG experience, as I have been depicting it, is an individual experience. Yet a note should be added to emphasize that Hopkins did not think of practical religion in strictly private terms. He was very much aware of, and alert to, the social realities in which a person must live, struggle, and find meaning. He could write at times, and with a surprisingly modern ring, of problems of pollution,[5] of increasing urbanization and the plight of the poor,[6] of early communism as he knew it,[7] and of what a true commonwealth would be like. Of Hopkins's wider concern with such societal needs as well as individual life, Alison Sulloway has a useful epitome: "His work reflects the anguish of religious strife, abuse of labor, the scandal of privileged cruelty, the horrors of rampant industrial-ism, pouring its scum and smoke all over England, the search for personal and national prescriptions, and above all, the anatomy of mental suffering."[8] Ultimate solutions, of course, are not simply social remedies, and divine grace is not dependent on the status of human institutions. But what human beings are called upon to do as part of earthly religion does involve heed to social institutions and as such serves at least as a background consideration in inter-preting Hopkins.

In the end, however, the confrontation with Hopkins's religious poetry must be an individual confrontation. It speaks to us indivi-dually with what is called existential relevance. It is not just that Hopkins introduces poetic innovations, skills with language, and the like, which after all are a literary legacy to culture, but rather that he speaks to our personal situation, perhaps better than we can ourselves. If we have known something of the pangs of encagement in our own lives, if we have known something of the struggles for self-mastery and productive effort, if we have experienced some-thing of the liberating bounty of freely given grace, then we will know whereof Hopkins speaks and will know that he speaks for us. And we will be grateful for this personal word of truth that has been spoken through the strange eloquence of his poetry.

To give an appraisal of Hopkins in this fashion is to depart from many a literary appraisal. In chapter six I commented on Yvor Winters's low estimation of Hopkins, and about this view I wish here only to add a further quotation from Thomas McDonnell which seems to me particularly apropos: "It is, I believe, a failure of the secular imagination to recognize the very real presence of the theological implications in Hopkins' poetry."[9] This comment points in the direction of the present interpretation.

Another literary appraisal that focuses more on linguistic elements than on intellectual statements is that of Austin Warren. Warren first divides Hopkins's poems into three classes: the early youthful poems, which follow Keats and the pre-Raphaelites; the middle poems from 1875 to 1885 (that is, from the *Wreck* to "Tom's Garland"); and the late sonnets, in which Hopkins "was a poet of tense, economic austerity."[10] Warren then declares (but without justification) that the middle poems are "the most Hopkinsian— the most specially his own."[11] And of these middle poems Warren writes: "To try prose paraphrases of the middle poems is invariably to show how thin the 'thinking' is. ... His reflections on beauty, man, and nature—his humanistic thoughts—are not distinguished."[12] With the middle poems being taken as "most Hopkinsian," and with the content of these being dismissed as superficial, the appraisal of Hopkins's poems is reduced to a case of interesting word-play: "The rewarding experience of concern with them is to be let more and more into words and their ways, to contemplate the protopoetry of derivation and metaphorical expansion, to stress the inscapes of the English tongue."[13]

I do not wish to minimize the linguistic and dictional significance of Hopkins's poetry or to minimize the meticulous, scholarly investigation of this topic which Professor Warren and others have done. But as an overall estimate of the total Hopkins, this appraisal is certainly a paltry one because it downplays the later poems, subordinates in general the content of the poems to linguistic and formal elements, and does not see the unifying themes in the poetry as a whole. Far different is the present appraisal which does include content as central and which does consider the "theological implications," as McDonnell puts it—or, as I might have put it, the experiential impact made possible by the poetic content.

My own appraisal might be charged with subjectivism—a charge that would be serious and in need of refutation. My view does claim to work outward from the poetry itself. Thus I can agree wholeheartedly with a criticism that Todd Bender makes of an early critical interpretation by I. A. Richards, but I would also insist that such a criticism does not apply to this view. Richards believed that art should bring about a certain physiological balance or poise in the organism and that poetry which does this is commendable. But of this view Bender writes:

> To praise Hopkins because the ambiguities of his verse create a state of mental poise is, of course, to divert critical interest from what went on in the author's mind when he wrote the poem to what goes on in the critic's mind when he reads the poem. Richards' praise implies a subjective approach to his poetry and indeed such an approach has been dominant ever since the second edition of the poems was printed.[14]

The alternative to focusing on the author's psyche or on the critic's psyche is simply to focus on the poetry—a naive assertion but one of which critics and scholars seem constantly to need reminding. My own approach has begun strictly with the poetry. I have claimed that the poetry of Hopkins exhibits a certain phenomenological structure, a certain phenomenology of religious experience. That this phenomenology is so is a feature of the poetry itself and is independent of whether Hopkins himself experienced it or whether the audience experiences it. If that phenomenology has been presented with poetic skill and power, then the poetry stands as significant poetry in itself. If then, besides this, the experience portrayed is a profound human experience, and if the account illuminates the experience of a significant number of fellow pilgrims, then one can claim that this ought to redound further to the greatness of the author of that poetic phenomenology. I do not think of this as a subjective approach but rather one that is open to scrutiny and evaluation by anyone who also enters into the poetry with empathy and knowledge.

We identify with our past cultural spokesmen—artists, philosophers, scientists, teachers, humanitarians, saints. Why do we do so? Doubtless many reasons are present in different cases. But one reason must surely be that these past spokesmen have said something significant, and said it significantly, to us individually. So it must be with Hopkins for those who feel any identification with him. The reason can seldom be external similarities in life, which are usually very scant. It must be rather that a poetic word of power has been spoken to a listening mind. Of such individual impacts are cultural contributions sometimes made.

Notes

NOTES, CHAPTER I

1. Todd K. Bender, *Gerard Manley Hopkins* (Baltimore: Johns Hopkins Press, 1966), pp. 34-35.
2. James Collins, "Philosophical Themes in G. M. Hopkins," *Thought*, 22 (March 1947): 67-106.
3. J. Hillis Miller, "Gerard Manley Hopkins," in *The Disappearance of God* (Cambridge: Harvard University Press, 1963), pp. 270-359.
4. Ross Snyder, "Phenomenology," The Chicago Theological Seminary *Register*, 61, no. 3 (March, 1971): 1.
5. Paul L. Mariani, *A Commentary on the Complete Poems of Gerard Manley Hopkins* (Ithaca and London: Cornell University Press, 1970), p. xx.
6. Yvor Winters, *The Function of Criticism* (Denver: Alan Swallow, 1957), p. 145.
7. Edward H. Cohen, "The Present State of Hopkins Scholarship," *The Hopkins Quarterly*, 1, no. 1 (April 1974): 20.
8. Thomas à Kempis, *The Imitation of Christ*, trans. Ronald Knox and Michael Oakley (New York: Sheed and Ward, 1959), Book II, Chap. 9, sec. 4. Subsequent quotations from this source will be cited in parentheses in the text by book: chapter, page.
9. Included by Christopher Devlin in *The Sermons and Devotional Writings of Gerard Manley Hopkins* (London: Oxford University Press, 1959), pp. 203-4. Devlin includes this section of the *Spiritual Exercises* as background in his edition of Hopkins's sermons and devotional writings. I follow his excerpt here because the terms "consolation" and "desolation" are retained instead of "comfort" and "discomfort." Later in this study I shall follow the Corbishley translation.
10. Ibid., p. 204. All quotations in the next two paragraphs are taken from this same page.

11.   Martin C. D'Arcy, Foreword, *Gerard Manley Hopkins: Priest and Poet*, by John Pick, 2nd ed. (New York: Oxford University Press, 1966), pp. vii-viii.

12.   W. H. Gardner, *Gerard Manley Hopkins; a Study of Poetic Idiosyncracy in Relation to Poetic Tradition*, 2nd ed. (London: Oxford University Press, 1961), 2: 330.

13.   Robert J. Andreach, *Studies in Structure: The Stages of the Spiritual Life in Four Modern Authors* (New York: Fordham University Press, 1964), Chaps. 1-2.

14.   Pick, *Hopkins*.

15.   A good place for doing this research is the Hopkins collection at Gonzaga University. See Ruth Seelhammer, *Hopkins Collected at Gonzaga* (Chicago: Loyola University Press, 1970).

16.   Katherine Bregy, "Gerard Hopkins: an Epitaph and Appreciation," *Catholic World*, 88 (January 1909): 445. Italics in this and all other quotations used in this book follow the original authors' actual usage.

NOTES, CHAPTER II

1.   These biographical details derive chiefly from the three volumes of letters, which I shall utilize in chapter five in the account of Hopkins's own experience.

2.   For this and all subsequent quotations from Hopkins's poetry, refer to W. H. Gardner and N. H. Mackensie, eds., *The Poems of Gerard Manley Hopkins*, 4th ed. Numbers in parentheses correspond to the poem-numbers in that collection. "The Caged Skylark" is number thirty-nine.

3.   *New Catholic Encyclopedia* (New York: McGraw-Hill Book Company, 1967), 4: 897.

4.   Ibid., p. 805.

5.   *Sacramentum Mundi: An Encyclopedia of Theology*, ed. Karl Raehner et al. (New York: Herder and Herder, 1968), 2: 69.

6.   Isaiah 45:15.

7.   *The New Catholic Edition of the Holy Bible*, a Revision of the Challoner-Rheims Version (New York: The Catholic Book Publishing Co., 1957).

8.   *The Living Bible* (Wheaton, Ill.: Tyndale House Publishers, 1971).

9.   The next eight quotations are from, respectively, the unnamed desolation sonnets numbered 65, 68, 61, 69, 65, 67, 69, and 67 in the *Poems*.

NOTES, CHAPTER III

1.   *The Letters of Gerard Manley Hopkins*, ed. Claude Colleer Abbott, 2nd ed. (London: Oxford University Press, 1955), no. 64 (25 October 1879), p. 95. Quoted in part in chapter five.

2. For some of Hopkins's drawings and scores that remain, see *The Journals and Papers of Gerard Manley Hopkins*, ed. Humphrey House (London: Oxford University Press, 1959), Appendix 1, pp. 453ff, and Appendix 2, pp. 457-97.
3. See Mariani, *Commentary*, pp. 178-81, for a beginning commentary on the poem.
4. From Hopkins's own headnote to the poem.
5. James Reeves, ed., *Selected Poems of Gerard Manley Hopkins* (London: Heinemann, 1953), note to the poem.
6. Reeves, *Selected Poems*, note to "The Starlight Night."
7. *Poems*, p. 109; also p. 111 and 176.
8. Reported by an intimate friend as quoted by G. F. Lahey in his 1930 biography, *Gerard Manley Hopkins* (New York: Octagon Books, 1970 reprint), p. 147.

NOTES, CHAPTER IV

1. *Sacramentum Mundi*, 2: 416.
2. See chapter seven, section three.
3. Some discussion of instress is given in chapter seven, section two.
4. Translated from the Latin by B. H. P. Farrer, as included in the notes to the poem, in *Poems*, p. 319.
5. J. Hillis Miller, "The Linguistic Moment in 'The Wreck of the Deutschland,'" in *The New Criticism and After*, ed. Thomas D. Young (Charlottesville: University Press of Virginia, 1976), p. 48. See also David A. Downes, "Grace and Beauty in 'The Wreck of the Deutschland,'" *Hopkins Quarterly*, 3 (January 1977): 139-55; and *Readings of the Wreck*, ed. Peter Milward, and Raymond V. Schoder, (Chicago: Loyola University Press, 1976).
6. This last stanza is the type of passage which prompted P. T. Geach in a conference lecture to chide Hopkins for the unacceptable practice of praying for the past. But see the interesting article by Michael Dummet, "Bringing about the Past," *The Philosophical Review*, 73, no. 3 (July 1964): 138-59, which alludes to praying about the past as part of a larger topic.
7. John Baillie, *Our Knowledge of God* (New York: Charles Scribner's Sons, 1959), p. 178.
8. Denes Donoghue, *The Ordinary Universe* (London: Faber & Faber, Ltd., 1968), quoted in Tom Dunne, *Gerard Manley Hopkins; a Comprehensive Bibliography* (Oxford: Clarendon Press, 1976), pp. 162-63, item H284.
9. T. S. Eliot, *After Strange Gods* (London: Faber & Faber, Ltd., 1934), quoted in Dunne, *Bibliography*, p. 134, item H49.

NOTES, CHAPTER V

1. *Further Letters*, Introduction, p. xxi.
2. Mariani, *Commentary*, p. xxii.
3. *Sermons*, dust jacket (1967 reprint).
4. *Sermons*, Introduction, p. xiv.
5. *Letters*, Introduction, p. v.
6. *Sermons*, Introduction to Part 3, pp. 214ff.
7. *Letters*, no. 100 (26 March 1883), p. 178.
8. *Letters*, no. 106 (26 July 1883), p. 183.
9. *Sermons*, p. 215.
10. Ibid., p. 217. The "weeks" mentioned here are not weeks in the retreat but divisions in Loyola's *Spiritual Exercises*. Hopkins's experience must have coincided with these.
11. *Sermons*, p. 253.
12. Ibid., p. 254.
13. *Sermons*, p. 217.
14. *Letters*, no. 129 (17 May 1885), p. 219.
15. *Letters*, no. 130 (1 September 1885), p. 221.
16. Ibid., pp. 221-22.
17. *Further Letters of Gerard Manley Hopkins, Including His Correspondence with Coventry Patmore,* ed. Claude Colleer Abbott, 2nd ed. (London: Oxford University Press, 1956), no. 98 (17 May 1885), p. 171.
18. *Letters*, no. 129 (17 May 1885), p. 216.
19. *Further Letters*, no. 140 (8 May 1885), p. 256.
20. *Sermons*, p. 218.
21. Ibid., p. 219.
22. *Letters*, no. 130 (1 September 1885), p. 221.
23. *Sermons*, p. 262.
24. Ibid.
25. Ibid., p. 263.
26. Ibid.
27. *Sermons*, p. 221.
28. Ibid., p. 261.
29. Ibid., p. 262.
30. *Further Letters*, no. 47 (16 October 1866), p. 95.
31. *Further Letters*, no. 28 (13 June 1868), p. 51. For a fuller documentation of Hopkins's melancholic disposition, including both earlier and later years, see David Downes, *Gerard Manley Hopkins: a Study of his Ignatian Spirit* (New York: Bookman Associates, 1959), pp. 114f.
32. *Letters*, no. 38 (25 February 1878), p. 47.
33. *The Correspondence of Gerard Manley Hopkins and Richard Watson*

Dixon, ed. Claude Colleer Abbott, 2nd ed. (London; Oxford University Press, 1956), no. 2 (13 June 1878), p. 9.

34. *Letters*, no. 53 (15 February 1879), p. 66.
35. *Further Letters*, no. 34 (15 June 1881), p. 62.
36. *Further Letters*, no. 136 (22 May 1880), p. 244.
37. *Letters*, no. 70 (26 October 1880), p. 110.
38. *Further Letters*, no. 139 (14 January 1883), p. 251.
39. *Letters*, no. 113 (16 April 1884), p. 192.
40. *Correspondence*, no. 32 (25 October 1884), p. 123.
41. *Correspondence*, no. 35 (8 August 1886), p. 139.
42. *Letters*, no. 146 (17 February 1887), pp. 250-51.
43. *Letters*, no. 157 (12 January 1888), p. 270.
44. *Letters*, no. 162 (18 August 1888), p. 278.
45. *Further Letters*, no. 140 (24 April 1885), p. 254.
46. Downes, *Study*, pp. 116-17.
47. *Journals*, pp. 131-263, covering years from 1866 to 1875.
48. "On the Origin of Beauty: A Platonic Dialogue," *Journals*, pp. 86-114.
49. *Letters*, no. 64 (25 October 1879), p. 95.
50. *Correspondence*, no. 10A (1 March 1880), p. 32. Italics Dixon's.
51. *Letters*, p. xxxviii.
52. *Poems*, p. xlviii.
53. *Further Letters*, no. 177 (4 April 1885), p. 359.
54. Ibid., p. 358.
55. *Further Letters*, no. 184 (20 January 1887), p. 377.
56. *Poems*, p. xxviii.
57. *Further Letters*, no. 168 (24 September 1883), p. 308.
58. *Letters*, no. 51 (19 January 1879), p. 61.
59. *Further Letters*, nos. 141-156 (1886), pp. 257-76.
60. *Further Letters*, no. 34 (15 June 1881), p. 62.
61. *Further Letters*, no. 136 (22 May 1880), pp. 244-45.
62. *Letters*, no. 159 (10 February 1888), pp. 273-74.
63. *Letters*, no. 171 (29 April 1889), p. 306.
64. *Further Letters*, no. 162 (1 May 1888), p. 290.
65. *Letters*, no. 52 (29 January 1879), pp. 63-64.
66. *Poems*, p. xxvii. Italics Gardner's.
67. Ibid., p. xxv.
68. C. Bowen, "Reminiscences of Father Gerard Hopkins," *Month*, 134 (August 1919): 158-59.
69. *Letters*, no. 171 (29 April 1889), pp. 303-4.
70. *Further Letters*, no. 127 (14 May 1881), p. 248.
71. *Correspondence*, no. 2A (25 September 1878), p. 10.
72. *Correspondence*, no. 22 (1 December 1881), p. 93.

73. *Correspondence*, no. 19 (12 October 1881), p. 75.

74. *Correspondence*, no. 34 (3 July 1886), pp. 137-38.

75. *Poems*, p. xxiii.

76. Mariani, *Commentary*, p. xxi.

77. Patrick O'Donovan, "The Tragedy of Gerard Manley Hopkins," *Observer Magazine* (18 August 1968), quoted in Dunne, *Bibliography*, p. 124, item G99.

78. C. N. Luxmoore to Arthur Hopkins (13 June 1890), in *Further Letters*, p. 396.

79. Letter dated 12 August 1889, quoted by Abbott in his Introduction to *Further Letters*, p. xxxvi.

NOTES, CHAPTER VI

1. John Wain, *Gerard Manley Hopkins: an Idiom of Desperation* (New York: Folcroft, 1959), p. 24.

2. Compare W. S. Johnson, *Gerard Manley Hopkins: the Poet as Victorian* (Ithaca: Cornell University Press, 1968), and Alison G. Sulloway, *Gerard Manley Hopkins and the Victorian Temper* (New York: Columbia University Press, 1972).

3. *Correspondence*, no. 19 (12 October 1881), p. 75.

4. *Correspondence*, no. 20A (26 October 1881), p. 80.

5. Herbert Read, "Poetry and Belief in Gerard Manley Hopkins," *New Verse*, 1 (January 1933): 15.

6. W. H. Gardner, *Study*, 1: 36.

7. *Poems*, Introduction, p. xxv.

8. Gardner, *Study*, 2: 339.

9. Robert J. Andreach, *Studies in Structure*, p. 9.

10. Ibid., p. 32.

11. Howard W. Fulweiler, *Letters from the Darkling Plain: Language and the Grounds of Knowledge in the Poetry of Arnold and Hopkins* (Columbia, Mo.: University of Missouri Press, 1972), p. 137.

12. Ibid., p. 163.

13. Elizabeth Sewell, "Humor and Hopkins," *Duckett's Register*, 5, no. 3 (March 1950): 41. This author is not supporting but only stating the view.

14. *See* pp. 121–22.

15. Alfred Thomas, "Gerard Manley Hopkins: 'Doomed to Succeed by Failure,'" *Dublin Review*, 240 (Summer 1966): 161.

16. David A. Downes, "The Hopkins Enigma," *Thought*, 36 (Winter 1961): 573. This author is not supporting but only stating this theory.

17. John Pick, "Gerard Manley Hopkins: the Problem of Religious Poetry," *The Stylus*, 55, no. 4 (February 1942): 20.

18. Martin C. Carroll, "Gerard Manley Hopkins and the Society of Jesus,"

in *Immortal Diamond*, ed. Norman Weyand (New York: Sheed and Ward, 1949), pp. 3-50.

19.   Alfred Thomas, *Hopkins the Jesuit: the Early Years of Training* (London: Oxford University Press, 1969).

20.   Downes, "Hopkins Enigma", p. 584.

21.   Carroll, *Society of Jesus*, p. 3.

22.   F. R. Leavis, "Gerard Manley Hopkins: Reflections after Fifty Years," (The Hopkins Society: second annual lecture, given at the University of London, 1 March 1971), p. 21.

23.   Yvor Winters, *Function of Criticism*, p. 153.

24.   Ibid., pp. 153-54.

25.   Ibid., p. 108.

26.   Theodore Weiss, *Hopkins: A Study in Romanticism* (M.A. thesis, Columbia University, 1940), p. 1.

27.   Theodore Weiss, "On Seeing a Portrait of Gerard Manley Hopkins," *Columbia University Quarterly*, 32 (December 1940): 332.

28.   Theodore Weiss, "Gerard Manley Hopkins: Realist on Parnassus," *Accent*, 5 (Spring 1945): 142.

29.   Ibid., p. 143.

30.   Ibid.

31.   Fulweiler, *Letters from the Darkling Plain*, p. 137.

32.   Patricia M. Ball, *The Science of Aspects* (London: the Athlone Press, 1971), Appendix.

33.   J. Hillis Miller, *Disappearance of God*, pp. 340-341.

34.   Ibid., p. 359.

35.   Ibid.

36.   E. Elizabeth Phare, *The Poetry of Gerard Manley Hopkins* (1933; reprinted New York: Russell and Russell, 1967), pp. 101f.

37.   Ibid., p. 101.

38.   Ibid.

39.   Ibid., p. 150.

40.   Robert R. Boyle, "The Teaching of Hopkins," *Jesuit Educational Quarterly*, 7, no. 2 (October 1944): p. 94.

41.   Lahey, *Hopkins*, p. 143.

42.   For a discussion of Boyle's view of Hopkins, see Fulweiler, *Letters from the Darkling Plain*, pp. 124f.

43.   *Letters*, p. xl.

44.   *Letters*, p. xxxviii.

45.   Lahey, *Hopkins*, p. 143.

46.   E. K. Taylor, "Gerard Manley Hopkins: a Poet for Priests," *Clergy Review*, 37 (July 1952): 402.

47. Geraldine Colligan, "The Mysticism of Hopkins," *Ave Maria*, 58 (November 1943): 591.
48. Ibid., p. 593.
49. Andreach, *Studies in Structure*, p. 5.
50. Evelyn Underhill, *Mysticism*, 12th ed. rev. (London: Unwin Brothers, Ltd., 1962), pp. 381-82.
51. Ibid., p. 415.
52. Andreach, *Studies in Structure*, Chaps. 1-2.
53. Frederick J. Streng, *Understanding Religious Man* (Belmont, Calif.: Dickenson Publishing Company, Inc., 1969), Chaps. 5-8.
54. Miller, *Disappearance of God*, p. 341.
55. Ibid.

NOTES, CHAPTER VII
1.   Downes, *Study*, p. 74.
2.   Gardner, *Study*, 1: 37.
3.   *Correspondence*, no. 38 (29 January 1887), p. 150.
4.   Vernon J. Bourke, *Ethics* (New York: The Macmillan Company, 1951, 1966), p. 399.
5.   Louis Dupre, "The Mystical Experience of the Self and its Philosophical Significance," *International Philosophical Quarterly*, 14, no. 4 (December 1974): 495.
6.   *Further Letters*, no. 136 (22 May 1880), p. 245.
7.   Gardner, *Study*, p. 13.
8.   *Correspondence*, no. 37 (23 October 1886), p. 146.
9.   *Poems*, Introduction, p. xxxv.
10. *Sermons*, p. 28. All subsequent references in this chapter to the *Sermons* will be cited in the text in this way: (*Sermons*, [page number(s)]).
11. *The Spiritual Exercises of St. Ignatius Loyola*, trans. Thomas Corbishley (Wheathampstead, Hertfordshire: Anthony Clarke Books, 1973), pp. 79-80.
12. Ibid., p. 22.
13. *Letters*, no. 53 (15 February 1879), p. 66.
14. *Further Letters*, no. 188 (7 November 1886), p. 373.
15. John Pick, *Hopkins*, p. 33.
16. Raymond V. Schoder, "An Interpretive Glossary of Difficult Terms in the Poems," in *Immortal Diamond*, ed. Norman Weyand (New York: Octagon Books, 1969), p. 199.
17. *Poems*, Introduction, p. xx.
18. Miller, *The Disappearance of God*, pp. 286-87.
19. Pick, *Hopkins*, p. 33.

20. Miller, *Disappearance of God*, p. 289.
21. *Spiritual Exercises*, p. 80.
22. *Journals*, p. 127.
23. *Letters*, no. 136 (13 October 1886), p. 231.
24. Isaiah 45:15.
25. *Poems*, Introduction, p. xxxvi.
26. Gardner, *Study*, 1: 51.
27. *Spiritual Exercises*, p. 22.
28. *Letters*, no. 99 (3 February 1883), p. 175.
29. *Spiritual Exercises*, p. 40.
30. Translation: "Man comes from God and must return to God. There are two movements in man: that of his divinely created being toward existence and that of his existent being toward God. These two movements are given to man by God; and by these two movements, man, if he wills, will return infallibly to God. I say if he wills, because man can change the direction of this movement." From *La Vie et les oevres de Maria Lataste*, Book i, sec. 5, included by Devlin in *Sermons*, p. 327.
31. Translated from the Welsh by Dr. T. Parry, *Poems*, p. 325.
32. Translation: "The past, the present and the future are for God only one and the same thing; for him, the future and the past are always present." From *Maria Lataste*, Book i, sec. 16, in *Sermons*, p. 328.
33. Miller, *Disappearance of God*, p. 272.
34. *Letters*, no. 97 (4 January 1883), p. 166.
35. Translation: "It is certain that God knows all from all eternity, and that he knows as a consequence those who will be rebels." From *Maria Lataste*, Book i, sec. 16, in *Sermons*, p. 328.
36. Translation: "But now, this foreseeing of God does not influence at all the reprobation of man, for it does not have any effect on man who retains all his liberty, and is able to ill-use or not ill-use the graces of God. ... It is because man causes his own fall that God foresees it, and not because God foresees it that man is lost and damned. God gives graces, but he leaves with them liberty, and man, in giving or refusing his assent to these graces, damns himself or saves himself freely." Ibid., p. 328.
37. *Spiritual Exercises*, p. 123.
38. *Journals*, pp. 118-21.
39. *Letters*, no. 64 (25 October 1879), p. 95.
40. Bender, *Hopkins*, pp. 64-5.
41. *Letters*, no. 133 (1 June 1886), p. 225.
42. Barbara Hardy, "Forms and Feelings in the Sonnets of Gerard Manley Hopkins" (Hopkins Society: first annual lecture given at University College, London, 12 February 1970), p. 4.

NOTES, EPILOGUE

1. W. H. Gardner, *Study*, 2: 330.
2. John Rawls, *A Theory of Justice* (Cambridge: Harvard University Press, 1971), p. 440.
3. Downes, *Study*, p. 78.
4. Gardner, *Study*, 1: 21-22.
5. *Letters*, no. 171 (29 April 1889), p. 299.
6. *Further Letters*, no. 161 (1 May 1888), p. 293.
7. *Letters*, no. 26 (2 August 1871) and no. 27 (22 January 1874), pp. 27-29.
8. Suloway, *Hopkins and the Victorian Temper*, p. 6.
9. Thomas McDonnell, "Hopkins as a Sacramental Poet: a Reply to Yvor Winters," *Renascence*, 14 (Autumn 1961): 28.
10. Austin Warren, "Instress of Inscape," in *Hopkins: a Collection of Critical Essays*, ed. Geoffrey H. Hartman (Englewood Cliffs, N.J.: Prentice-Hall, Inc., 1966), p. 168.
11. Ibid.
12. Ibid., p. 177.
13. Ibid.
14. Bender, *Hopkins*, p. 19.

Bibliography

This bibliography is limited to books that have some special relevance to the present study. Some relevant articles are cited in footnotes.

Writings of Hopkins

The Poems of Gerard Manley Hopkins. 4th ed. Edited by W. H. Gardner and N. H. Mackenzie. London, Oxford, and New York: Oxford University Press, 1967.
The Letters of Gerard Manley Hopkins to Robert Bridges. 2nd ed. Edited by Claude Colleer Abbott. London: Oxford University Press, 1955.
The Correspondence of Gerard Manley Hopkins and Richard Watson Dixon. 2nd ed. Edited by Claude Colleer Abbott. London: Oxford University Press, 1955.
Further Letters of Gerard Manley Hopkins, Including His Correspondence with Coventry Patmore. 2nd ed. Edited by Claude Colleer Abbott. London: Oxford University Press, 1956.
The Journals and Papers of Gerard Manley Hopkins. Edited by Humphrey House. London: Oxford University Press, 1959.
The Sermons and Devotional Writings of Gerard Manley Hopkins. Edited by Christopher Devlin. London: Oxford University Press, 1959.

Bibliographical Works

Cohen, Edward H. *Works and Criticism of Gerard Manley Hopkins: a Comprehensive Bibliography*. Washington, D.C.: The Catholic University of America Press, 1969.

Dunne, Tom. *Gerard Manley Hopkins: a Comprehensive Bibliography*. Oxford: Clarendon Press, 1976.

Seelhammer, Ruth. *Hopkins Collected at Gonzaga*. Chicago: Loyola University Press, 1970.

Books on Hopkins, in Whole or Part

Andreach, Robert J. *Studies in Structure: The Stages of the Spiritual Life in Four Modern Authors*. New York: Fordham University Press, 1964.

Bender, Todd K. *Gerard Manley Hopkins*. Baltimore: Johns Hopkins Press, 1966.

Cotter, James Finn. *Inscape: The Christology and Poetry of Gerard Manley Hopkins*. Pittsburgh: University of Pittsburgh Press, 1972.

Downes, David A. *Gerard Manley Hopkins: a Study of his Ignatian Spirit*. New York: Bookman Associates, 1959.

Fulweiler, Howard W. *Letters from the Darkling Plain: Language and the Grounds of Knowledge in the Poetry of Arnold and Hopkins*. Columbia, Mo.: University of Missouri Press, 1972.

Gardner, W. H. *Gerard Manley Hopkins; a Study of Poetic Idiosyncracy in Relation to Poetic Tradition*. 2nd ed. 2 vols. London: Oxford University Press, 1949.

Hartman, Geoffrey H., ed. *Hopkins: a Collection of Critical Essays*. Englewood Cliffs, N.J.: Prentice-Hall, Inc., 1966.

Heuser, Alan. *The Shaping Vision of Gerard Manley Hopkins*. London and New York: Oxford University Press, 1958.

Hunter, James. *Gerard Manley Hopkins*. London: Evans Brothers, Ltd., 1966.

Johnson, W. S. *Gerard Manley Hopkins: the Poet as Victorian*. Ithaca: Cornell University Press, 1968.

Kenyon Critics. *Gerard Manley Hopkins*. London: Dennis Dobson, Ltd., 1949.

Lahey, G. F. *Gerard Manley Hopkins*. 1930. Reprint. New York: Octagon Books, 1970.

Mariani, Paul L. *A Commentary on the Complete Poems of Gerard Manley Hopkins*. Ithaca and London: Cornell University Press, 1970.

McChesney, Donald. *A Hopkins Commentary*. London: University of London Press, 1968.

MacKenzie, Norman H. *Hopkins*. Edinburgh and London: Oliver and Boyd, 1968.

Miller, J. Hillis. *The Disappearance of God; Five Nineteenth Century Writers*. Cambridge: Harvard University Press, 1963.

Peters, W. A. M. *Gerard Manley Hopkins: a Critical Essay Towards the Understanding of his Poetry*. 2nd ed. 1948. Reprint. Oxford and New York: Basil

Blackwell and Johnson Reprint Corporation, 1970.

Phare, E. Elizabeth. *The Poetry of Gerard Manley Hopkins.* 1933. Reprint. New York: Russell and Russell, 1967.

Pick, John. *Gerard Manley Hopkins: Priest and Poet.* 2nd ed. New York: Oxford University Press, 1966.

Sulloway, Alison G. *Gerard Manley Hopkins and the Victorian Temper.* New York: Columbia University Press, 1972.

Weyand, Norman, ed. *Immortal Diamond: Studies in Gerard Manley Hopkins.* 1949. Reprint. New York: Octagon Books, 1969.

Winters, Yvor. *The Function of Criticism.* Denver: Alan Swallow, 1958.

Index